THE
FLOWER
ARRANGER'S
ENCYCLOPEDIA
OF PRESERVING
AND DRYING

FLOWERS FOLIAGE SEEDHEADS
GRASSES CONES LICHENS FERNS
FUNGI MOSSES

THE FLOWER ARRANGER'S ENCYCLOPEDIA OF PRESERVING AND DRYING

FLOWERS   FOLIAGE   SEEDHEADS
GRASSES   CONES   LICHENS   FERNS
FUNGI   MOSSES

Maureen Foster
Illustrated by Bryan Foster

BLANDFORD

A BLANDFORD BOOK

First published in the UK 1988
by Blandford
(a Cassell imprint)
Villiers House, 41/47 Strand, London, WC2N 5JE

Reprinted 1992

Distributed in the United States
by Sterling Publishing Co., Inc.
387 Park Avenue South, New York, NY 10016-8810

Distributed in Australia
by Capricorn Link (Australia) Pty Ltd
PO Box 665, Lane Cove, NSW 2066

British Library Cataloguing in Publication Data

Foster, Maureen
   The flower arranger's encyclopedia of
   drying and preserving.
   1. Dried flower arrangement
   I. Title
   745.92   SB449.3.D7

ISBN 0 7137 1899 4 *(hardback)*
ISBN 0 7137 2310 6

Typeset by Butler & Tanner Ltd, Frome and London
Printed in the U.K. by Bath Press

CONTENTS

Anemone coronaria

INTRODUCTION

When deciding some fifteen years ago to write my first book *Preserved Flowers, Practical Methods and Creative Uses,* I did so because at that time little had been written on this specialised aspect of flower arranging and I felt that such a book would serve as a useful reference for all the various plants which the flower arranger could dry or preserve, together with the most suitable methods of preserving them. Since that time I have written six other books dealing with the many aspects of this decorative art form and it has given me much pleasure to have had the opportunity of sharing many of my original ideas with my readers.

My decision to write yet another book comes as a result of the many enquiries and requests I have received for *Preserved Flowers,* of which the second edition has now been out of print since 1980. Over a period of fifteen years I have continued to discover many more plant materials that dry or preserve well and are interesting or decorative enough to add to my list. I have also become better acquainted with many of my original favourites and am now more acutely aware of the intricate forms and textures of many less colourful plant materials such as seedheads, cones, and grasses, many of which I find truly remarkable sculptures of nature, as you will see. I also find that preserving foliage has enabled me to make a closer study of the many interesting shapes of leaves. Words alone could not possibly convey these qualities, but I am fortunate that my husband is an artist and it is his patience and considerable skill that have enabled me to illustrate my text with beautifully detailed drawings which go to show what a remarkable designer nature is. Over 250 flowers, leaves, grasses, seedheads, cones, ferns fungi, mosses and lichens are illustrated, with detailed descriptions of each one, together with what I find to be the most suitable methods of drying or preserving them.

I appreciate that not all flower arrangers have large gardens; in fact many will have no gardens at all. This fact I have kept very much in mind while compiling my book. Apart from common wild plants, I have included flowers that can be purchased from the florist, most of which are well known to us all. However, reference to interesting plant forms, such as lotus lily seedheads and the flower of the banksia, may seem strangely unfamiliar to readers in Britain. As natives of such countries as North America and Australia, plants such as these are imported and can often be purchased from the florist.

Although primarily an encyclopedia for the flower arranger, I hope that my book will encourage many readers not only to dry and preserve plant materials for long-lasting arrangements, but to take a closer look at the many wonders of nature which I feel all too often pass unnoticed when we are arranging fresh flowers.

The book is divided into alphabetical sections to enable immediate reference to be made when deciding if a particular flower, leaf or seedhead, etc., is suitable for preserving. This also enables the reader to select from a particular section of plant materials without having to cope with the all too familiar A–Z reference in which each plant description must be studied in depth to discover whether it is valuable for its flowers, leaves, seedheads or whatever.

Although I intend the book to be a complete reference work of drying and preserving, it is obvious that with the many thousands of plants, trees and shrubs, together with their countless varieties, available throughout the world, a totally comprehensive book would be an impossible task. However, I hope that reference to the illustrations and the accompanying text will make it possible to relate many plants to other similar forms.

In addition to the illustrations, the eight pages of colour have enabled me to illustrate several of my own arrangements in which I have used a wide range of plant materials. I hope these will encourage readers to create arrangements which are not only colourful but more closely resemble fresh arrangements, thus avoiding that typically dried look.

PLANT NAMES

Many flower arrangers feel they would rather avoid Latin names; they wonder why, for example, it is necessary to call a forget-me-not by the name of myosotis, when everyone knows it as a forget-me-not. Well, forget-me-not happens to be a generally accepted name, but many plants are known by more than one common name, and common names also tend to vary in different parts of Britain, and even more so in different parts of the world. However, if we stop to consider the names we use to describe our plants, we will realise that for many we already do use the Latin names – chrysanthemum and rhododendron are just two examples, for these, like many other plants, have no common name. It is for reasons like these that I have used the Latin names throughout the book as they have international recognition. However, readers who are not familiar with any of these can look up the common name which gives a quick reference to the appropriate botanical name.

1 FLOWERS

Including flowering catkins, flower-like bracts
and flower-like calyces

As flowers provide the most important source of colour for arrangements, it is important
to understand fully which types of flowers preserve successfully and by which method.
More than 50 per cent of the flowers I have described will retain their shape and form
when dried naturally by the air method. These include the annual everlasting flowers
(pages 45–49) which can be grown from seed especially for drying. With the description
of each plant I have given details including harvesting and the method of preservation
for flowers with which I have had personal success. When you have experimented with
some of these, experience will teach you the types of flowers to choose for preserving
to ensure successful results. Unfortunately, there are certain flowers which, due to the
thin texture and size of their petals, are not suitable. More details of these can be found
on page 143.

FLOWER-LIKE CALYCES Some plants appear to produce flowers with firm and exceptionally long-lasting petals.
Although often brightly coloured these are in fact not petals at all, they are petaloid
sepals (petaloid means like a petal). These form the calyx of the flower. Often tiny florets,
which are usually quite insignificant, will be found in the centre of these sepals. After
the florets have faded, the sepals mature and become firm. In fact, some become almost
paper-like, and this is an indication of the stage of growth at which they should be
gathered for successful preservation. If allowed to remain on the plant too long after
maturity the colour will be lost. In the group of plants known as Labiates, instead of
being petal-like, the calyx is joined and is bell- or trumpet-shaped, enveloping each
individual floret. The following are just a few of the plants which produce flower-like
calyces: moluccella, stachys, phlomis, ballota, hydrangea and hellebore. Descriptions of
these and others are included in the following section on flowers.

INFLATED CALYCES Botanically these should be included in the seedhead section, for they contain the seeds
of the plants. But their appearance, and the way in which I suggest they can be adapted
to resemble flower-like forms, make it necessary for me to include them in this section.
The flowers of these plants are relatively small and insignificant, but when the flowers
fade the calyx becomes inflated. This means that, unlike the calyces described above, the
sepals are joined. This inflated calyx contains the fruit of the plant which is in the form
of a spherical berry containing many seeds. I have only included two such plants, nicandra
and physalis (Chinese lantern).

FLOWER-LIKE BRACTS There are a few daisy-type flowers which have beautiful gleaming silvery bracts; these
are produced by the group of Compositae plants. With some of these plants it is not
until the flowers have withered and died that the attractive bracts are revealed, themselves
forming a flower-like shape of unique and outstanding beauty. The following are just a
few of the plants which produce flower-like bracts: *Centaurea nigra,* carline thistle and
catananche. Descriptions of these are included in the following section on flowers.
Note: Unless stated otherwise, the natural stem of the flower will be sufficiently firm
without the need for wiring.

ACANTHUS
BEAR'S BREECHES

This stately hardy perennial produces 90–120 cm (3–4 ft) spikes of purple-hooded white flowers which protrude like tongues from spiny green bracts. It is summer-flowering.

HARVESTING AND PRESERVING Gather when the lower flowers are fully mature regardless of whether or not the flowers at the top of the spike are open. Alternatively, the mature white flowers can be gathered from the ground where they are to be found at regular intervals during the flowering season, having been forced off by the development of large oval seeds. These white flowers can later be used with the striped seed spikes to make more elegant and graceful flower spikes.

Remove the seeds and the somewhat shrivelled purple flower hoods, leaving an uncluttered stem of firm bracts which in itself is quite beautiful and adds interest to an arrangement. To make this bracted stem into an elegant flower-spike, just dab glue on the base of each flower and sit them in the hollows of the bracts. This idea which I have recently developed produces a superior flower-spike, of an uncluttered and less 'dried' appearance. The striped seed spikes alone make an interesting feature in an arrangement.

Preserve using air method No. 1 or No. 2.

ACHILLEA
YARROW

The various species of this plant are all native to Europe. Of all the flowers that are suitable for drying or preserving, this summer-flowering hardy perennial possesses all the essential qualities necessary to ensure successful results with every flower. Their tightly packed heads of minute florets enable them to retain their form regardless of atmospheric conditions. When dry, their long, naturally stiff stems remain firm and rigid, and they also retain their true colourings.

The individual forms of achillea differ greatly.

A. filipendulina 'Coronation Gold' and 'Cloth of Gold'

These produce large flat plate-like heads on long straight, almost woody, stems. Each head comprises masses of minute florets of a beautiful golden yellow.

A. millefolium 'Fire King' and 'Cerise Queen'

These achilleas, although producing flattish heads, are smaller and in fact more divided than *filipendulina* and therefore less plate-like, but their pinkish red colouring makes them extremely useful for arrangements needing colour. Other varieties similar in form are 'Clyeolata', yellow, and 'Flowers of Sulphur' white.

There is also a wild variety of *A. millefolium* which grows by roadsides in the country and on waste ground in towns and cities. The white form is particularly common and flowers throughout the late summer and autumn. Less common in the wild is the pink form.

A. ptarmica
SNEEZEWORT

Two varieties very useful for preserved work are 'The Pearl' and 'Perry White'. Both have heads of double white flowers which are individually borne in quite large sprays. The flowers of 'Perry's White' are much larger than those of 'The Pearl'.

HARVESTING AND PRESERVING Gather as soon as all the tiny flowers have opened. After this stage I find they quickly begin to discolour. Preserve *A. filipendulina* and *A. ptarmica* using air method No. 1 or No. 3. Although *A. millefolium* will respond to these methods, I only use them if large quantities are needed as the dried heads tend to have that typically dried appearance. Instead I prefer to use the desiccant method as I find it produces preserved flower heads which retain their shape and form and differ little from their fresh counterparts. The remarkable stiff straight stems, together with the large plate-like heads, of *A. filipendulina* make these particularly suitable for line arrangements. Small sections of tiny florets can be taken from the heads of *A. filipendulina* or *A. millefolium* for use in miniature arrangements, or in the case of *A. ptarmica,* individual florets can be used.

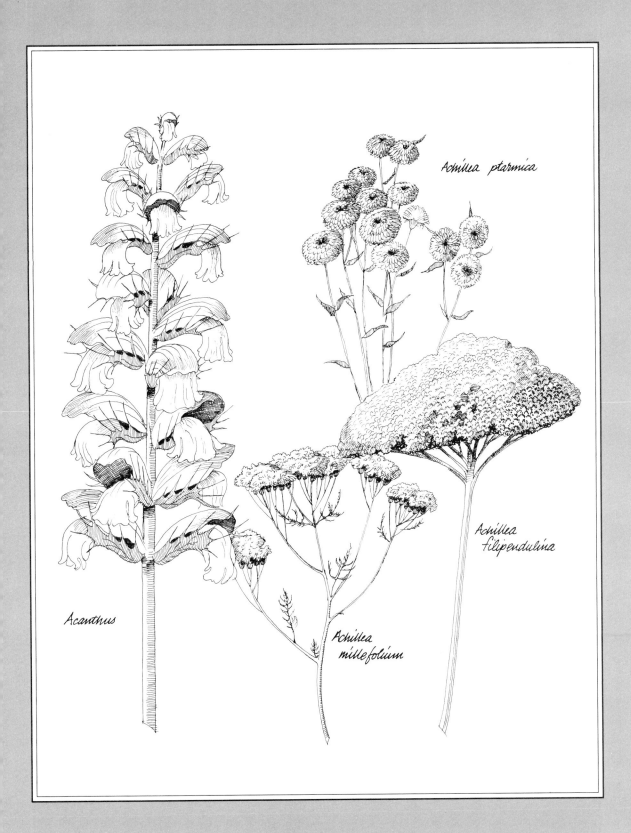

Achillea ptarmica

Achillea
filipendulina

Acanthus

Achillea
millefolium

ACONITUM
A. napellus
MONKSHOOD

From a distance this summer-flowering hardy perennial could be mistaken for a delphinium owing to its tall spike-like form. Each spike bears many florets which differ from those of the delphinium, being distinctly helmet-shaped. There are several varieties available, including 'Blue Sceptre', blue and white; 'Bressingham Spire', violet blue; 'Newry Blue', deep blue, and 'Spark's Variety' deep violet-blue.

HARVESTING AND PRESERVING Gather when the lower florets are mature, regardless of whether or not the top buds are open. Preserve using desiccant method No. 4, positioning.

AEGOPODIUM
A. podagraria
GROUND ELDER

This is one of a large group of wild plants which produce, in late spring and early summer, the characteristic white umbelliferous flower heads often referred to as 'Queen Anne's Lace'. In recent years I have found ground-elder to be the most successful, due to its firmer stems which, when preserved, are more able to support the flower heads. Reference to a comprehensive book of wild flowers will show many more umbelliferous plants several of which are worth experimenting with.

HARVESTING AND PRESERVING Gather mature flowers only and preserve using desiccant method No. 1, positioning.

USES Charming even when used alone without the addition of other plant materials, and exquisite when seen against a dark background, such as black or midnight blue.

AGERATUM
A. houstonianum
syn. **A. mexicanum**
FLOSS FLOWER

There are several varieties of this popular dwarf, half-hardy annual, summer-flowering, bedding plant, including many hybrids. With the exception of 'Spindrift' which has white flowers, all the other varieties I know have blue flowers in shades varying from light blue to a blueish mauve. It is these I value for preserving, revealing their truly lace-like quality.

HARVESTING AND PRESERVING Gather when the flowers are fully developed, which can be over a considerable period of time due to their long flowering period. Preserve using desiccant method No. 1, positioning.

USES Small and miniature arrangements.

ALCHEMILLA
A. mollis
LADY'S MANTLE

An easily grown hardy herbaceous plant of spreading habit, producing large open branched heads of minute star-like lime green florets in multiple clusters during summer. These exceptionally dainty flowers provide a contrast to the more solid forms of many other flowers.

HARVESTING AND PRESERVING The flowers have no true petals. What appear to be petals are in fact petaloid sepals which form the calyx of the flower. With maturity the minute pinhead-size flowers fade and appear as little dark centres within the calyx—which then becomes firm and therefore will retain its shape and form when preserved by air method No. 2, and also its lovely lime-green colouring. Picked at the same stage of growth and preserved using glycerine method No. 2, will result in beautifully supple heads of a deep olive green.

ALDER CATKINS   *see ALNUS GLUTINOSA*

Ageratum noustonianum

Alchemilla mollis

Aegopodium podagraria

Aconitum napellus

ALLIUM Most alliums are valuable for their seedheads, but two in particular provide colourful flowering heads which dry well. The summer-flowering vegetable-garden chives, *Allium schoenoprasum*, provide small pinky-cerise compact globular heads which are ideal for small arrangements. *Allium sphaerocephalium*, often listed in catalogues as 'Drumsticks', is a decorative form of allium with slightly larger heads than the chives. Its compact drumstick heads are deep purple-red; The large globular heads of the vegetable-garden leek provide very decorative flower heads which vary in colour from pale mauve to a somewhat greenish mauve. Leeks can also be dried later at seed stage (see page 88).

HARVESTING AND PRESERVING Gather before the flower heads are fully open, and dry by air method No. 1 or No. 2. Because of the large amount of moisture in their succulent stems, they will continue to open as they dry.

ALNUS GLUTINOSA—CATKINS *see CONE SECTION (page 109)*

ALTHAEA
A. rosea
HOLLYHOCK Some catalogues list the hollyhock as a hardy annual and some as a perennial, but in my summer garden over the years it has proved to be a natural hardy biennial. Having first grown the seeds many years ago, they continue as self-sown seedlings and I accept and enjoy their towering spikes wherever they happen to appear. Transplanted seedlings do not seem to produce such fine flower spikes.

I consider the flowers of the old-fashioned cottage-garden single varieties to be of far greater value in preserved work, for although the flowers of the double strains are very beautiful, I feel they have little character as preserved flowers. As a cut flower the hollyhock is of little use, as each stem, while producing many flowers, does so over a long period of time, and as a result only a few flowers are actually open at any one point. In fact the lower flowers fade and seed cases form before the top flowers open. For this reason the flowers of the hollyhock can be gathered over quite a long period of time. But while doing so, make a closer study of these individual blooms, for I am sure that to many of us their real beauty often passes unnoticed.

COLOURS White is perhaps the most beautiful of all, as its centre is a lovely limey-green radiating into yellow. The yellow and pink shades are also good, but the red is rather dull and a little disappointing after preservation.

HARVESTING AND PRESERVING Gather the buds as they begin to unfurl, and the more developed flowers as they reach cup-shape stage. Avoid fully opened blooms when they become almost saucer-shape, as at this stage they tend to be rather floppy when preserved. Ensure that each flower retains its little nodules of stem. After preserving by desiccant method No. 3, positioning, false stems will need to be attached to each flower (see page 153).

AMARANTHUS
LOVE-LIES-BLEEDING This summer-flowering hardy annual is sometimes better known as the tassel flower, owing to its long drooping tassels. *A. candatus* is deep maroon red, and, although much of this colour is retained after preserving, I find it a little drab and prefer the beautiful subtle green shade of *A. viridis* which develops definite yellow undertones when preserved.

HARVESTING AND PRESERVING Gather when the tassels are fully developed. Remove all leaves and use air method No. 2. *A. viridis* also responds well to glycerine method No. 2 which keeps the tassels beautifully supple.

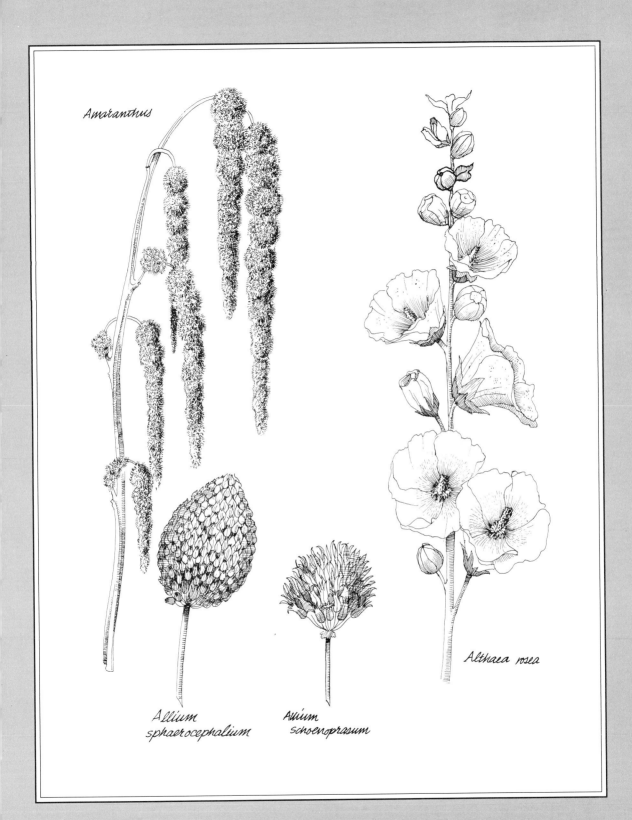

Amaranthus

Allium
sphaerocephalium

Allium
schoenoprasum

Althaea rosea

ANAPHALIS
PEARL EVERLASTING

Unlike the everlasting flowers described on page 45, the anaphalis is a hardy perennial. There are several varieties which vary in height, but all have the characteristic clusters of small pearl-white florets which appear in late summer. Each of these florets has a tiny golden eye which darkens as the flower reaches maturity. Later it turns fluffy and eventually falls out. Although smaller, the individual florets slightly resemble those of the annual everlasting ammobium, although each petal is narrower and of a softer texture.

HARVESTING AND PRESERVING Gather before the flowers are fully open. Preserve using air method No. 1.

USES Arrangements. Even flowers gathered after maturity make an additional form after the fluffy centres have been pulled out.

ANEMONE
WIND FLOWER

A. coronaria
POPPY ANEMONE

Within this group I find the most successful for preserving is the St Brigid anemone which, in spring, has single flowers in shades of red, cerise and blue with contrasting dark velvety centres and almost black stamens. During the winter months these anemones are readily available from florists.

A. elegans
JAPANESE ANEMONE

The various forms of Japanese anemones, in white and shades of pink, are all herbaceous plants, flowering in late summer to mid autumn.

HARVESTING AND PRESERVING Gather partially open flowers while the petals are still curved and overlapping. The petals tend to flop if left to open out completely flat. Wire before preserving (see page 145). Preserve using desiccant method No. 2, positioning.

USES Small arrangements.

ANTHEMIS

A group of summer-flowering hardy perennials with single daisy-like flowers which provide the ideal shape for anyone making a first attempt at preserving flowers in a desiccant.

A. cupaniana

This sub-shrubby perennial forms large mats of silvery grey foliage, and produces white flowers with deep yellow centres. These are ideal for preserving.

A. tinctoria
OX-EYE CHAMOMILE

There are many varieties which all preserve well. Examples are 'Grallagh Gold', 'Perry Variety' and 'Wargrave Variety', all of which produce yellow flowers, of varying shades, on stiff stems.

HARVESTING AND PRESERVING Gather at all stages, from buds just opening through to fully opened flowers. Preserve using desiccant method No. 1, positioning.

ASTILBE

This hardy perennial is often confused with aruncus (goat's beard) and filipendula (meadowsweet) both of which are of similar form and can be found in the seedhead section (pages 90, 96) as it is for their seedheads that these particular plants are valuable. The astilbe, which also provides good seedheads, is pretty at its flowering stage, in late summer, which is when I like to preserve it. Particularly good are the varieties which have red or pink flowers. There is also a pretty dwarf variety called *A. chinensis* which has pinkish-mauve flowers, preserves well and retains its colour.

HARVESTING AND PRESERVING Gather before the lower part of the flower loses its colour. Preserve using the desiccant method.

ASTRANTIA
A. maxima
MASTERWORT

This summer-flowering hardy perennial produces interesting rather than colourful flowers, with cushions of tiny dull pinkish or whiteish florets surrounded by papery bracts. The name astrantia is derived from *astron,* meaning a star, which aptly describes its star-like appearance.

HARVESTING AND PRESERVING Gather open flowers. Although these will dry well by air method No. 1, due of course to the firm papery flower bracts, the open flowers do tend to close up. I consider this to be an ideal method of drying large quantities of flowers, but if, like me, you prefer to preserve a few flowers which will retain their attractive open form, then I would suggest using the desiccant method.

Anemone coronaria

Anthemis
tinctoria

Astilbe

Anaphalis

Astrantia
maxima

BABY'S BREATH *see GYPSOPHILA*

BALLOTA
B. pseudo-dictamnus

Possibly more uncommon than most of the labiate family of plants this summer-flowering hardy perennial produces arching and often twisting stems which, from my personal experience, people have often mistakenly identified as pipe cleaners which does aptly describe their texture. Although almost hidden by the woolly-textured leaves, it is the flower-like calyces for which this plant is valuable. They grow in tightly packed whorls which encircle the stem at intervals, each surrounding a tiny insignificant floret.

HARVESTING AND PRESERVING Gather when all the flowers are out and beginning to fade. At this stage the calyces will be firm enough to hold their shape after preserving. They respond well to air method No. 1 (remove the leaves before or after). However, in time they do tend to become rather brittle unless carefully handled. For this reason I prefer to preserve them by glycerine method No. 2, to ensure the calyces remain supple and firmly attached to the stem. If this method is used, the leaves should be removed before preserving to economise on glycerine.

USES An ideal plant form with which to outline the curve of an arrangement.

BANKSIA

The genus Banksia which contains some fifty species and is found throughout Australia gets its name from the famous English naturalist Sir Joseph Banks. Each large dense inflorescence is estimated to contain more than 1,000 tiny flowers.

HARVESTING AND PRESERVING Fresh banksia flowers are often available from the florists in the spring. They can be dried by the air method either in flower, or after the flowers have faded although of course at this stage they will be rather drab.

BEAR'S BREECHES *see ACANTHUS*

BELLS OF IRELAND *see MOLUCCELLA*

BELLIS
B. perennis
DAISY

Known to Britain as the common lawn daisy or meadow daisy, in the USA it is commonly called the English daisy. This spring and summer-flowering lawn weed is one of the most successful and beautiful of all miniature preserved flowers.

CULTIVATED FORMS Many cultivated double forms of the daisy are available, which are spring-flowering and can easily be grown from plants or seeds. Among these 'Red Buttons' or 'Pomponette' have compact domed heads which preserve beautifully, but there are other equally good varieties which produce crimson, rose or white flowers. I find, with age, some plants revert, producing single flowers which have the dear little yellow eye of the lawn daisy. I am always thrilled when this reverting process occurs in the red and pink varieties.

HARVESTING AND PRESERVING Gather at any time from the bud stage to the fully mature flower. Preserve using desiccant method No. 1 for fully open flowers; No. 2 for those partially open, or buds.

USES Small and miniature arrangements. It may be necessary to strengthen the stems with a wire before arranging (see page 152).

BLADDER CAMPION *see SILENE*

CAPE GOOSEBERRY *see PHYSALIS*

CARLINA
C. acaulis
CARLINE THISTLE

On a recent holiday in northern Yugoslavia, I found this much larger stemless form of carline thistle. Set in rough grass on a sunny slope, its large flower heads measured as much as 12 cm (5 in) across, and with its silvery bracts shining in the hot sunshine, it appeared quite unreal, as though it had just been placed on its rosette of spiny leaves rather than actually growing there. I have since found it listed in Britain as a garden plant.

C. vulgaris

An interesting, rather than colourful, wild flower which can be found on dry calcareous grassland where, on sunny days, it can be easily recognised by its gleaming shiny straw-coloured bracts which surround a central boss of tiny florets. Beware, as with all thistles the leaves are extremely prickly.

HARVESTING AND PRESERVING Gather on a sunny day for only then are the bracts fully open. These flowers are at their best for drying before the centre turns fluffy. Use air method No. 1 or No. 2.

CALLUNA *see ERICA*

CARNATION *see DIANTHUS*

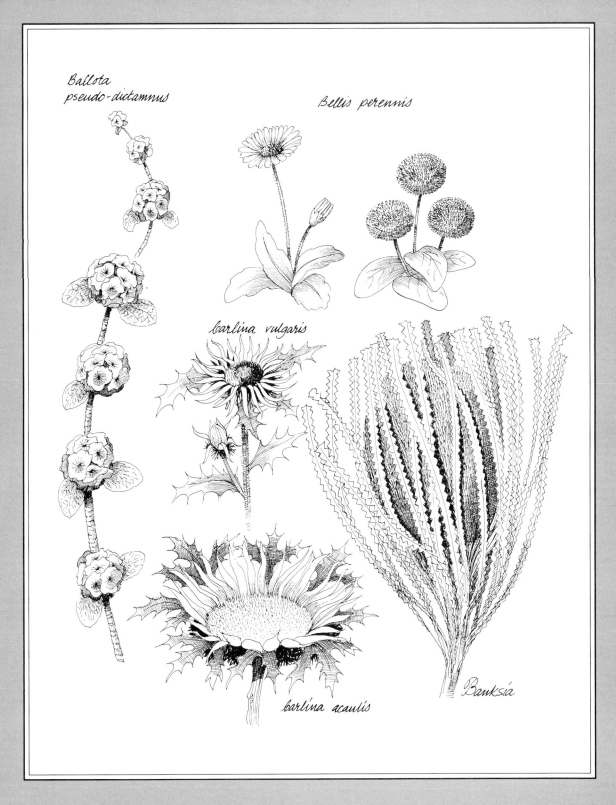

Ballota
pseudo-dictamnus

Bellis perennis

Carlina vulgaris

Carlina acaulis

Banksia

CATANANCHE
C. coeula
CUPID'S DART

This summer-flowering hardy perennial is often described in seed catalogues as an everlasting flower, although this is somewhat misleading. True everlastings are flowers in which the inflorescence consists of a central boss with no distinct petal shapes and surrounded by papery brightly coloured petal-like bracts. The catananche has bright blue daisy-like flowers which have distinctive petals surrounded by almost transparent colourless papery bracts.

HARVESTING AND PRESERVING If gathered when the flowers are open, they can only be successfully preserved by desiccant method No. 1 or No. 2, depending on how far open they are. Although this contradicts many seed catalogues, I find they can only be treated as everlastings and preserved by air method No. 1 or No. 2 if gathered after the flower petals have faded and fallen, at which time the bracts will close up, forming a colourless transparent and papery bud-like head.

CENTAUREA
KNAPWEED

This is a large group of plants which include hardy annuals, perennials and wild plants. I will describe the ones which I have found to be the most interesting and successful for preserving.

C. cyanus
CORNFLOWER

This is an excellent flower to grow for smaller arrangements, each plant producing masses of double flowers. Several named varieties are available of which 'Julep' and 'Polka Dot' are both good mixtures, containing shades of blue, mauve, crimson, rose-pink and white. The blue shades are particularly outstanding when preserved, and, with the addition of a little silver foliage, you need nothing more to make a striking miniature or petite arrangement. The mauve, rose-pink and white shades are also good, but the crimson, however, darkens to almost black, which of course is not uncommon with flowers of this shade.

HARVESTING AND PRESERVING Although satisfactory results can be obtained by preserving flowers at any stage of growth from bud to fully opened blooms, I have found partially opened flowers are best as they retain their compact form. Preserve using desiccant method No. 2, positioning. Reinforcing with a wire before preservation is advisable.

C. mactacephala
GLOBE CENTAUREA

Growing tall and erect during early summer, this interesting hardy perennial produces large globular heads of yellow thistle-like flowers surrounded by rich brown chaffy bracts.

HARVESTING AND PRESERVING Before they open, and while the buds are still tightly closed, the bracted heads can be dried by air method No. 1. Later during the early summer, when the heads open to reveal their yellow thistle-like flowers, they can also be dried by air method No. 1 or desiccant method No. 2, positioning. They even provide an interesting form later in the season when the flower has withered and become brown and flattened on the persistent bracted head. These too can be dried by air method No. 1.

C. nigra
COMMON KNAPWEED

This plant can be found growing wild throughout Britain in rough grassland. It has tall branching stems of mauve cornflower-like flowers. After the flowers have faded and fallen, persistent firm bracts remain. So common and yet so beautiful are these flower-like heads, but only when open. In late summer or early autumn they are most noticeable by roadsides when, on a dry sunny day, they open out to reveal their beautiful gleaming silvery insides. If gathered while open, they will remain so. When closed, however, their brown heads can aptly be described by their common name of hardhead. Dry by air method No. 1 or No. 2.

CHINESE LANTERN *see PHYSALIS*

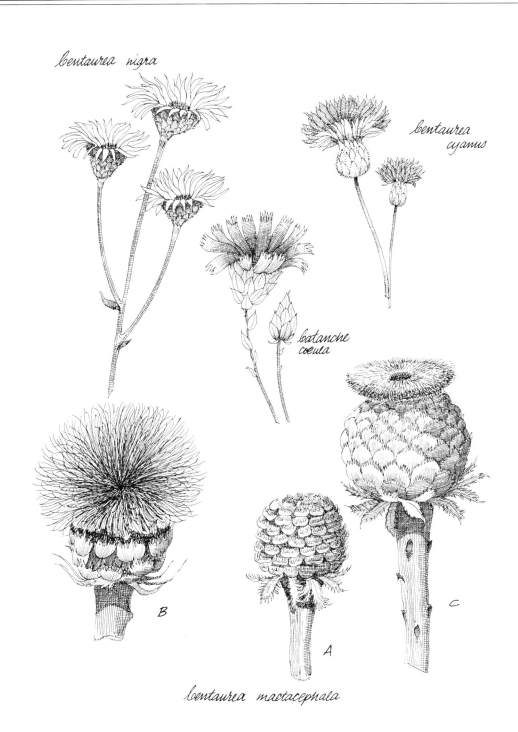

Centaurea nigra

Centaurea cyanus

Catanche coeula

B

A

C

Centaurea macrocephala

CHRYSANTHEMUM When the name chrysanthemum is mentioned, we usually think only in terms of the flowers on sale at the florist, or the ones gardeners grow for autumn flowering. Most of these are not suitable for preserving, the exception being the Pompon varieties which have heads closely packed with short overlapping petals, but even with these it is advisable to select the smaller flowers. Some of the dwarf varieties provide flowers small enough for miniature arrangements.

HARVESTING AND PRESERVING Select flowers in which the centres are not fully open to ensure they do not shatter when preserved. Use desiccant method No. 2, positioning.

C. parthenium
syn. **Matricaria eximia**
FEVERFEW

Also listed under the name of pyrethrum, this plant, with its aromatic leaves, is really a biennial which seeds itself year after year, producing 30–60 cm (1–2 ft) branched stems of single daisy-like white flowers with large golden yellow eyes. I also have a semi-double form called 'White Bonnet' which has white flowers with a small pale yellow eye. Two perennial dwarf varieties which readily seed themselves and are often sold as half-hardy annual summer bedding plants are 'Golden Ball' and 'Ball's Double White'.

HARVESTING AND PRESERVING When in full bloom all varieties are at their best for preserving. Preserve using desiccant method No. 1, positioning.

C. vulgare
syn. **Tanacetum vulgare**
TANSY

Flowering from late summer till early autumn, this hardy perennial is believed to be a garden escapee that has become naturalised in the wild. Once cultivated as a herbal and medicinal plant, it is still grown as a garden plant. Although I find it rather rampant, the large flattish yellow flower heads are useful for late colour in the garden, as well as for drying.

HARVESTING AND PRESERVING Gather when fully open, and dry by air method No. 1.

NOTE Even after the colour has faded and the heads have turned brown, they still provide a useful form for preserved arrangements.

CLARY *see SALVIA*

CORYLUS
C. avellana
HAZEL

In early spring, the pendulous golden yellow catkins of the common hazel are a welcome sight after the long dull days of winter. These catkins, which are about 5 cm (2 in) long when fully mature, are in fact the male flowers of the hazel. They form in clusters of two, three and four on the leafless twigs.

HARVESTING AND PRESERVING I have found these preserve most successfully if gathered earlier in the year; late January or February is the ideal time. The catkins will of course be less conspicuous at this time, as they will be greyish in colour and remain firm and tightly closed, but if preserved by glycerine method No. 1, after a week or so they will have extended in length and will open, release their pollen and become beautifully supple.

NOTE During the preserving process it is advisable to place a paper under the container to catch the pollen. When removed from the container the catkins should be taken out of doors and given a good shake to remove any remaining pollen.

C. avellana 'Contorta'
CORKSCREW HAZEL

The curious twisted branches of this unusual cultivated hazel hold a fascination for all flower arrangers, and, when gathered complete with catkins, they have added appeal.

HARVESTING AND PRESERVING Early in the year these leafless contorted branches can be preserved with or without their catkins in the same way as *C. avellana*.

NOTE It may seem unnecessary to preserve bare branches, but if, like me, you have to travel some distance to visit a friend who grows this hazel, it is extremely useful to be able to keep the branches for many months without them drying out and becoming brittle.

COTTON LAVENDER *see SANTOLINA*

DAFFODIL *see NARCISSUS*

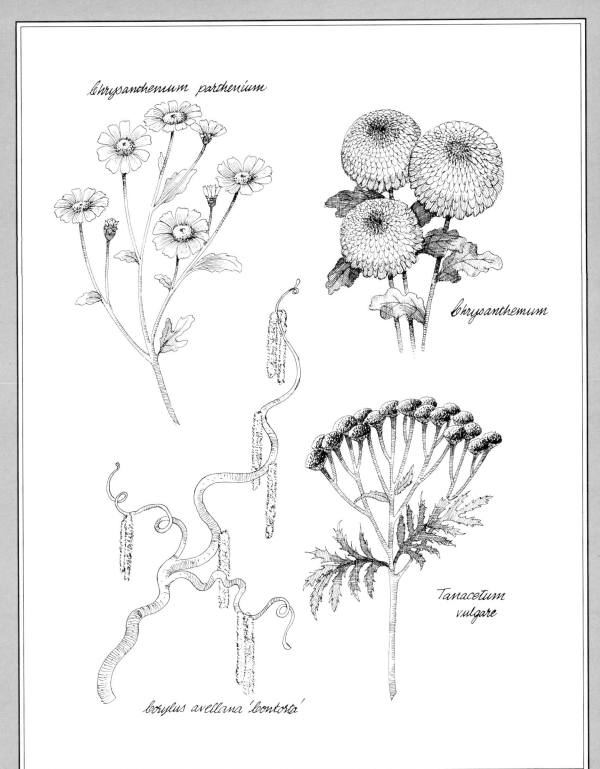

Chrysanthemum parthenium

Chrysanthemum

Tanacetum vulgare

corylus avellana 'contorta'

DAHLIA The National Dahlia Society have divided the modern hybrid dahlias into ten classes, each comprising many varieties. Only two of these classes provide varieties which are ideal for preservation. These are the Decorative and Pompon. The class of Decorative dahlias is sub-divided into five sections according to the size of the blooms. It is the two sections of small and miniature varieties that I find most satisfactory.

In both the Decorative and Pompon classes can be found varieties in a wide selection of colours, most of which preserve well. These include shades of yellow, orange-bronze, white and mauve, together with vibrant reds which have yellow undertones. Reds with blue undertones will almost certainly darken, this being characteristic of this shade in all flowers, which means that many of the darker red and purple shades will become too dark when preserved to be of any real value.

HARVESTING AND PRESERVING In late summer, gather mature flowers that show no signs of wilting, preferably before the last few petals of the flower have opened and revealed the yellow centre. Wilting first becomes evident in the first petals that open, the ones nearest the calyx on the back of the flower. Insert wires for false stems (see page 145) and preserve using desiccant method No. 2, positioning.

DAISY *see BELLIS*

DELPHINIUM This hardy perennial is a particularly good flower for preservation, and, with careful handling, can provide some excellent flower spikes for arrangements. I suggest you first experiment with the side shoots which you will find easier to handle than the main stem. Many named varieties are available in shades of blue, of which I find those with smaller flowers are more suitable for preserving than the large-flowered hybrids. There are also pink and white varieties which preserve well, but if I had to choose I would always favour the blue shades, especially as there are so few blue flowers of this size. The contrasting black eyes, so characteristic of many varieties, look like little black bees and give the preserved blooms added appeal.

D. ujacis
LARKSPUR This popular hardy annual can be grown from seed. The flowering spikes of blue, pink, rose and white are also available from florists during the summer months.

HARVESTING AND PRESERVING Gather stems before the lower flowers fade. Due to the length of the delphinium's main stem it is generally only practical to dry these by the air method No. 1 or No. 3. However, in my opinion delphiniums dried by this method come into the category of 'typically dried'. I much prefer to wait until the side shoots develop as these are not only easier to handle but their length fits more conveniently into a standard biscuit tin, which enables them to be more successfully preserved by the desiccant method No. 4. After preserving the stems may be lengthened as shown on page 152.

DIANTHUS
CARNATION The dianthus family includes Alpine and border pinks, sweet Williams and the perpetual double greenhouse carnations. It is the latter that I recommend as a flower for preserving, as both the large flowered varieties and the smaller flowered spray carnations all have double flowers with closely packed petals, and all are readily available from the florist throughout the year. The reason for preserving carnations will usually be one of sentiment because of their commercial popularity as a predominant flower in wedding bouquets, corsages and many other special-occasion tributes. Most colours preserve well although white is inclined to take on a rather grey look and the dark red tends to become very dark, unless it is a bright red with yellow undertones.

HARVESTING AND PRESERVING Make quite sure that the petals are all flat, this being an indication of the flower's freshness. If the flower is past its best each tiny petal will curl up, giving the flower a somewhat shrunken appearance. Use desiccant method No. 2, positioning. After preserving, the petals often become loose in the calyx, giving the flower head a rather open effect. If this happens, wiring can be effectively used to tighten the head. Simply bind a fine silver wire around the calyx just under the petals where it will be concealed.

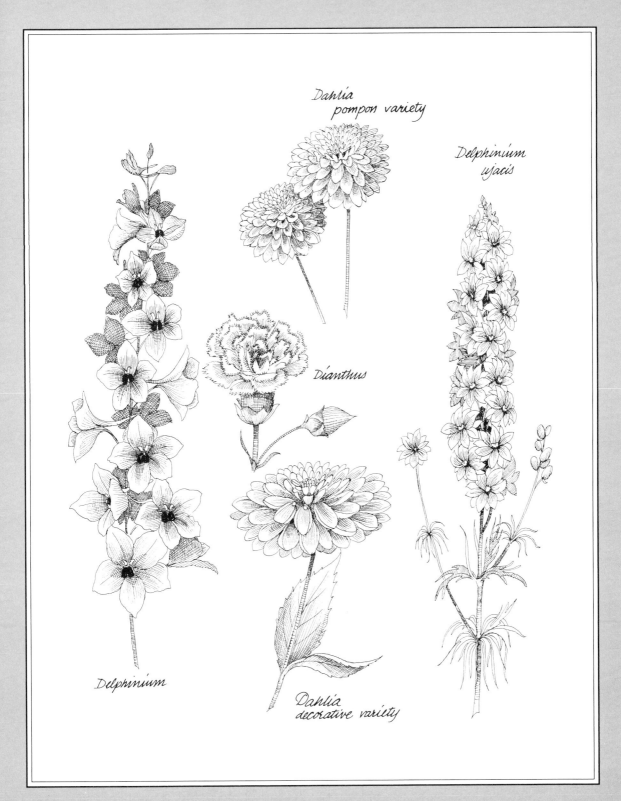

Dahlia
pompon variety

Delphinium
ajacis

Dianthus

Delphinium

Dahlia
decorative variety

ECHINOPS
E. ritro
GLOBE THISTLE

Valuable for its globular heads of spiky steel-blue bracts which open to provide blue globular flower heads, these summer-flowering hardy perennials give both an unusual shape and an interesting shade. The name echinops is derived from the Greek word *echinos,* a hedgehog, and *opis,* like, which is a very apt description.

HARVESTING AND PRESERVING Success of preservation will depend *entirely* on the stage of growth at which this flower is harvested. I have tried picking the spiky ball before the flowers open, and also after they have faded, both without success. It is only when the last flowers have opened on the ball (these being the ones nearest the stem) that the globe thistle will preserve without disintegrating. Use air method No. 1 or No. 2.

NOTE The leaves of the echinops also preserve well and are particularly decorative (see page 60).

ELDER

see SAMBUCUS

ERICA
HEATH or HEATHER

In British gardens we can grow both summer- and winter-flowering heaths, or heathers as they are often better known. There are white varieties and pink varieties which include many really deep, almost red, shades. Although these are typical hardy perennial plants for an acid soil, varieties of *E. carnea* and *E. darleyensis* will tolerate some lime in the soil. American readers will find varieties of heather available from florists during the non-gardening season.

The summer-flowering bell heathers that grow wild on acid soils in many parts of Britain, particularly on heathland, all preserve well, although I must say I have a preference for the dainty characteristic form of the wild ling, *Calluna vulgaris.* This differs from the bell heather, as each small floret has four tiny mauve-pink petals which give it a more delicate appearance.

HARVESTING AND PRESERVING Gather when fully out but before the lower florets fade. Use air method No. 4. When completely dry, shake well to remove all the tiny loose brittle leaves.

ERYNGIUM

An interesting group of plants, the flowers of which are excellent for both fresh and preserved arrangements due to their distinctive flower heads which appear in late summer.

E. alpinum
'Donard'

The flower head is similar to that of *E. giganteum,* but the metallic-blue bracts are finely divided and not spiny.

E. giganteum

Known as Miss Wilmott's ghost, this eryngium has a large teasel-like head with minute blue flowers, surrounded by a collar of broad spiny bracts which are a beautiful silvery grey. After flowering, the eryngium dies, but readily reproduces itself from self-sown seedlings.

E. maritimum
SEA HOLLY

A typical wild plant of coastal sand-dunes, with small teasel-like heads of minute blue florets and broad grey green bracts. The eryngium's common name of sea holly adequately describes this plant as the spiny bracts resemble a holly leaf and are extremely prickly.

E. tripartitum

A small, decorative, but less striking, form of eryngium with small flower heads carried on branching stems.

HARVESTING AND PRESERVING Gather when fully open by which time the bracts will be firm. Use air preserve method No. 1 or No. 2.

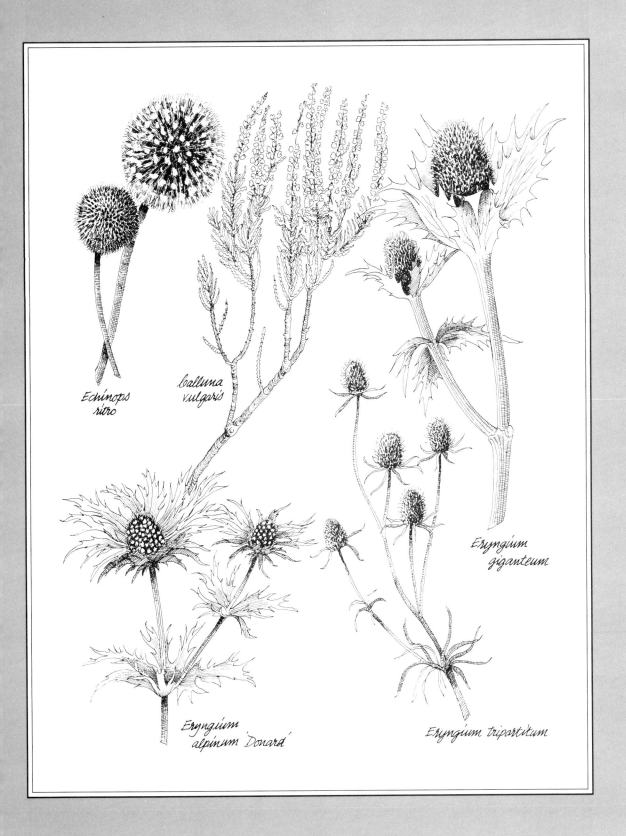

Echinops
ritro

Calluna
vulgaris

Eryngium
giganteum

Eryngium
alpinum 'Donard'

Eryngium tripartitum

EUPATORIUM
E. cannabinum
HEMP AGRIMONY

This tall perennial wild plant is widespread and common throughout most of England and Wales, but becoming less common in the north. It grows in large clumps of up to 120 cm (4 ft) in height and is found mainly in wet ditches, marshes and damp woods where its large dense flower heads, in a subtle shade of pink, provide a showy mass of colour from mid-summer till early autumn. Hemp agrimony is the only British species of eupatorium, but there are others which grow wild in North America where they are common plants of the same damp conditions. One in particular, which is similar to *E. cannabinum,* is perhaps better known by its common name of Joe-Pye weed.

HARVESTING AND PRESERVING Gather when the flowers are in bud and they will continue to open as they dry. If picked later when the flowers have opened, the heads will become a fluffy mass and are not so colourful. Dry using air method No. 1. Remove foliage.

FEVERFEW *see CHRYSANTHEMUM PARTHENIUM*

FORGET-ME-NOT *see MYOSOTIS*

FREESIA

Its exquisitely perfumed trumpet-shaped flowers are a firm favourite among florists' flowers. Freesias are now available in a wide range of colours including white, lavender blue, cerise-pink and yellow. In wedding bouquets they are as popular, if not more so, than the carnation and not only their colour, but their form, preserves remarkably well.

HARVESTING AND PRESERVING Take complete sprays with buds and fully open flowers, or individual buds and flowers. Preserve using desiccant method No. 3, positioning. Both single and double varieties preserve well.   USES Small arrangements.

FREMONTODENDRON
syn. Fremontia
F. californicum
FLANNEL BUSH

This is a Californian tree or large shrub which retains its leaves throughout the winter, but needs to be planted against a sheltered wall to ensure its survival. Its large golden yellow calyxed flowers consist of five large overlapping sepals, for the fremontia has no petals. There is also a very vigorous hybrid listed, 'Californian Glory', which is a cross between the above shrub and *F. mexicanum.* This fremontia is described as being even more valuable because of the size of its flowers and the greater production of them over a long season.

HARVESTING AND PRESERVING This flower is particularly successful for preserving due to the firm texture of its calyx, although I do find the colour retention a bit unpredictable. Most flowers retain their true colour, but some darken and a few bleach to a beautiful pale parchment colour. But whatever the final colour, I find them extremely beautiful and useful. Preserve using desiccant method No. 2, positioning.

FUCHSIA
F. hybrida

A group of flowering shrubs which are natives chiefly of Central and South America. There are many, many, varieties of fuchsia under cultivation, some of which are hardy, but most are tender and need either to be grown in a greenhouse or at least given greenhouse protection during the winter. The flowers are composed of a tube, with four spreading sepals attached, hanging from the centre of which is the corolla. In some varieties the corolla is beautifully frilled and always reminds me of a ballerina's skirt. These are usually the varieties with a short tube and I feel these are the most attractive as a preserved flower, especially for use in arrangements.

HARVESTING AND PRESERVING Gather fully open flowers and preserve by desiccant method No. 2, positioning.

GARRYA
G. elliptica
SILK TASSEL BUSH

A native of California, *Garrya elliptica* is much prized by the flower arranger for its grey-green pendulous flowering catkins. From a preservation point of view I consider this to be a dual purpose shrub, for it is valuable not only for its catkins, but also for its tough glossy leaves which you will find listed on page 66.

HARVESTING AND PRESERVING This is a subject on which to concentrate early in the year. Wait until the catkins are open and fully expanded as they are most attractive at this stage. This is usually between late January and March. At such a time it is possible to preserve the catkin-bearing branches in full leaf, for *G. elliptica* is evergreen. For ease of arranging it is often advisable to preserve separate branches of leaves and catkins, in which case it will be necessary to strip the leaves from the branches of catkins, before preserving by glycerine method No. 1.

GLOBE THISTLE *see ECHINOPS*

GOLDEN ROD *see SOLIDAGO*

GROUND ELDER *see AEGOPODIUM*

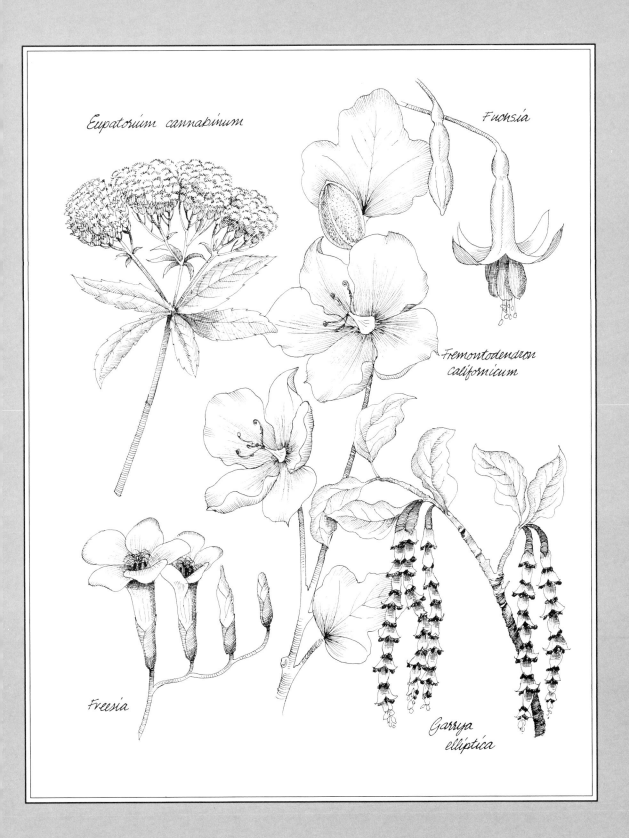

Eupatorium cannabinum

Fuchsia

Fremontodendron californicum

Freesia

Garrya elliptica

GYPSOPHILA
G. paniculata
BABY'S BREATH

I am delighted that this hardy perennial is now back in fashion particularly in wedding bouquets. I consider the best variety for preserving to be 'Bristol Fairy' which produces masses of tiny double florets in large branching panicles, creating a cloud-like effect. Gypsophila is readily available from the florist and is particularly charming when used with the more solid forms of summer flowers such as dahlias and roses. This enables a true 'summer garden in winter' arrangement to be created.

HARVESTING AND PRESERVING Gather when fully developed and all the flowers are open. Use air method No. 1 or No. 2.

HEATH or HEATHER *see ERICA*

HELLEBORE *see HELLEBORUS*

HELLEBORUS
H. orientalis
HELLEBORE
LENTEN ROSE

This spring-flowering hardy perennial is a most successful flower for preservation due to the firm texture of its petal-like sepals. Varying in colour considerably, from a greenish-cream, pink, or pinkish-mauve, these sepals are often mistaken for the petals of the hellebore, but in fact the hellebore has no petals.

HARVESTING AND PRESERVING Fully developed flowers can be picked complete with their beautiful cluster of stamens. They can also be gathered later when, with maturity, the sepals, unlike petals, will not drop but will, in fact, have toughened considerably. Although by this time their colouring will have become more muted, and tiny seedpods will have developed, they will still be attractive and their flower form will often be longer lasting when preserved.

H. niger
CHRISTMAS ROSE

I delight in preserving a few of these each year for the sheer beauty of their smooth white flowers which, if left in the garden unprotected, soon become damaged by severe winter weather conditions as they open.

HARVESTING AND PRESERVING To make quite sure I have perfect blooms for preserving, I usually pick buds and allow them to open indoors by standing them in a container of water. Preserve using dessicant method No. 2, positioning.

HOLLYHOCK *see ALTHAEA*

HYDRANGEA
H. macrophylla
COMMON HYDRANGEA

These summer-flowering shrubs are normally divided into two groups, Lace Caps, and mop heads known as Hortensia. The Lace Caps I feel have little decorative value when preserved, but varieties of Hortensia, in their many varying shades, are invaluable. These are the hydrangeas with large globular heads consisting of many small flowers which appear to have long-lasting petals. In fact these are not true petals but petaloid sepals, which is the reason for their longevity. The minute insignificant florets, which are sterile, can be found in the centre of these sepals.

HARVESTING AND PRESERVING The most successful time to gather and preserve hydrangeas is in the autumn. At this time of year the sepals on most of the heads will have become firm and should feel slightly papery to the touch. Unfortunately the colours will have changed, but the more subtle shades I find equally, if not more, attractive. For example, the vibrant blue becomes steel-blue, sometimes tinged with pink, the delicate shades of pink become a soft green, while deeper pinks turn burgandy where the heads are fully exposed to the light, and green on the parts which are underneath and shaded. The longer it is possible to leave these flower heads, the more successfully they will preserve. Remove the leaves and preserve using air method No. 4.

NOTE If it is preferable or necessary to preserve hydrangea heads at an earlier stage of growth, the desiccant method should be used.

JERUSALEM SAGE *see PHLOMIS*

KNAPWEED *see CENTAUREA*

LADY'S MANTLE *see ALCHEMILLA*

LARKSPUR *see DELPHINIUM*

LAVANDULA
L. spica
LAVENDER
OLD ENGLISH LAVENDER

This small evergreen shrub needs no introduction as it is so reminiscent of old English cottage gardens where it is said to have been first introduced in 1568. It is a native of the Mediterranean regions. The name Lavandula is derived from the Latin *lavare,* meaning to wash, which refers to its use in the preparation of lavender water.

Although all varieties preserve well, I find the deep blue of *Nana atropurpurea,* often known as 'Hidecote', more colourful for arrangements.

Gypsophila
paniculata

Helleborus
orientalis

Hydrangea
macrophylla

Lavandula
spica

LAVANDULA
L. spica
LAVENDER
OLD ENGLISH LAVENDER

HARVESTING AND PRESERVING I like to gather the flower spikes in full bud, just before the dark blue calyces open and the tiny flowers peep out, as it is the calyces that are particularly colourful and dry without any deterioration. If picked later, the tiny flowers tend to fade and, like other labiates, they really need to be pinched out to avoid producing what is in my opinion a rather tatty, typically dried specimen which would be ideal for pot-pourri or lavender bags, but not for arrangements. Preserve by air method No. 1 or No. 3. It is more effective when grouped in small bunches rather than as single stems.

LAVENDER see LAVANDULA

LENTEN ROSE see HELLEBORUS

LIATRIS
L. spicata
BLAZING STAR

This hardy late-summer-flowering herbaceous perennial has tall spikes of purplish flowers. Although a native of North America, the liatris has become more widely known in both Britain and North America as a garden plant. It is also popular with florists in both countries as a cut flower.

HARVESTING AND PRESERVING The flowering spikes of the liatris have the unusual habit of opening from the tip downwards, making it necessary to pick them for drying before the tip begins to wither, regardless of whether or not the lower flowers on the spike have opened. Use air method No. 1.

LILAC see SYRINGA

LILIUM
LILY

Possibly the most beautiful of all bulbous plants, as a flower for preserving the lily may be considered unsuitable due to the fleshiness of its petals. In fact this used to be so, when only products like borax and sand were available for use as preserving agents, but, with the introduction of more efficient desiccants, many varieties now preserve and retain their colour and form remarkably well. Particularly good varieties to choose are those with orange or yellow flowers such as 'Harmony' and 'Destiny', which are usually readily available from the florist. To me lilies seem to create a feeling of elegance and grandeur, and yet are economical to use. For readers who have to rely on the florist for their sole supply of flowers for preserving, a single stem carrying some five or six blooms will usually be adequate for a striking long-lasting line arrangement. Flowers such as lilies I like to refer to as feature flowers because they are important enough to use on their own with a suitable foliage.

HARVESTING AND PRESERVING Select a good stem and immediately cut off and preserve individual flowers that are open at the time of purchase. Keep the stem with the remaining buds standing in water and then, one by one, wire and preserve the flowers as they open. Preserve using desiccant method No. 3, positioning. If petals become loose or flop, refer to page 150.

LOVE-IN-A-MIST see NIGELLA

MASTERWORT see ASTRANTIA

MARIGOLD see TAGETES

MATRICARIA EXIMIA see CHRYSANTHEMUM PARTHENIUM

MOLUCCELLA
M. laevis
BELLS OF IRELAND

Also called the shell flower because of the stems of green shell-shaped calyces which make this plant so valuable and decorative.

HARVESTING AND PRESERVING It is essential to wait until the tiny insignificant flowers within the calyces have bloomed and faded, by which time the calyces will be mature and firm with an almost papery feeling to them. Should the growing season not be long enough to enable the top few inches of stem to mature, this can easily be pinched out after preserving, at which time it will probably have become noticeably floppy. These can be preserved by air method No. 1, but they are inclined to become rather brittle, and so I prefer to use glycerine method No. 2.

MONKSHOOD see ACONITUM

MONTBRETIA see CROCOSMIA

MYOSOTIS
FORGET-ME-NOT
M. alpestris

There are many named varieties in shades of pink and blue, including a very deep indigo blue, and even a white form is available. Although all of these are excellent for preserving, it is the blue shades which I find most valuable for miniature arrangements. Not only is it one of our few true-

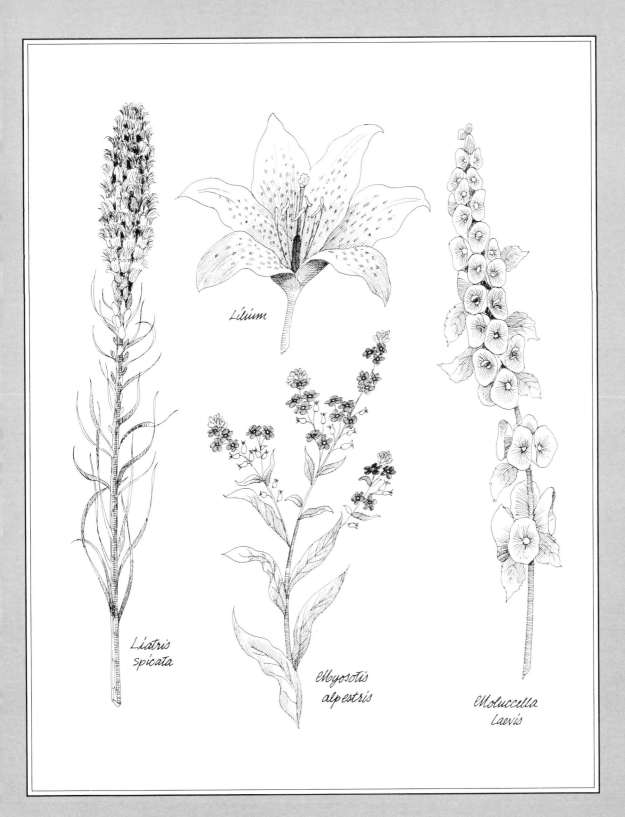

Lílium

Líatris
spicata

Myosotis
alpestris

Moluccella
Laevis

MYOSOTIS
FORGET-ME-NOT
M. alpestris

blue tiny flowers, but somehow I only really like to associate forget-me-nots with shades of blue. I leave some plants each year to seed themselves and, as they do so very freely, I am never without masses of self-sown seedlings of delightful blue forget-me-nots.

HARVESTING AND PRESERVING Do not attempt to preserve forget-me-nots until the seed vessels have formed for about 2–5 cm (1–2 in) up the stems. At this stage the stems and petals of the remaining florets will be much firmer. They can in fact be gathered at any time after this, right up until the last few flowers open at the tip of the stem. Preserve by desiccant method No. 1, positioning.

USES Small and miniature arrangements. To produce a greater impact of colour in arrangements, try wiring several stems together after preserving. Remove the seed vessels.

NARCISSUS
DAFFODIL

There are so many varieties in this large group of spring-flowering bulbs that it is only possible for me to give a guide to the most satisfactory type of blooms to preserve. Regardless of whether they are trumpet daffodils or cup-shaped varieties, miniature or large-flowered, I find it is the petals which are the deciding factor, and I suggest selecting varieties with relatively short wide over-lapping petals, which are of a firm texture.

HARVESTING AND PRESERVING Gather when the flowers are fully developed. Replace the stems with florist's wires (see page 145).

SPECIAL NOTE Leave a length of stem on the flower and insert the wire into this, pushing it up carefully until it pierces the ovary, but while doing this be careful to keep the paper-like sheath intact.
    Preserve using desiccant method No. 2 positioning.

USES Arrangements, ideal for associating with wood, moss, fungi and lichen.

NICANDRA
N. physalodes
APPLE OF PERU

An unusual but vigorous summer-flowering half-hardy annual which also has the common name of shoo-fly, as it is probably supposed to repel flies. The attractive pale violet flowers of nicandra are bell-shaped and measure 4 cm (1½ in) or more across. As these fade, quite large dry globular berries form, each contained within a bright green and purple inflated calyx. These are similar in shape to physalis (page 36) to which they are closely related.

HARVESTING AND PRESERVING Gather in late summer when the calyces are fully formed and mature, at which time they will feel papery to the touch but should still retain their colouring. Remove the leaves and dry by air method No. 1. When completely dry, each calyx can be made into an interesting flower-like form simply by cutting through each of the five ribbed seams and opening up each section to form a delicately veined 'petal'. It will be possible, if you so wish, carefully to remove the thin dry covering of the berry and shake out the seeds to reveal an attractive intricate centre for your 'flower'.

NYMPHAEA
WATER LILY

A large group of summer-flowering aquatic plants which include the hardy water lilies. There are miniature varieties, such as N. pygmaea, N tetragona and N. candida, which are ideal for small pools or tubs, and larger and more vigorous varieties, such as N. gladstoniana, which are more suited to larger ponds and lakes. Regardless of size they all produce flowers in shades of white, pink, yellow and red, which have a beautiful sculptured quality. The yellow, white and pale pink shades preserve well, but I find the red a little disappointing.

HARVESTING AND PRESERVING Gather the flowers when fully open, usually about midday on a sunny day. Cut each flower with about 5 cm (2 in) of stem. As the water lily usually rests on the surface of the water, the backs of the petals will need to be dried, but do keep an eye on it, for, as evening approaches, the petals begin to close, and, alas, it may be too late to preserve your treasured bloom as it may not open again the next morning. When dry, reinforce the succulent stem as shown (see page 146). Preserve using desiccant method No. 2, positioning. Because of the fleshiness of the petals, I suggest allowing three weeks for water lilies to preserve, after which sealing is recommended (see page 151).

USES Arrangements. The beauty and charm of the water lily, in my opinion, needs nothing more than to be arranged on a flat dish with its own leaves which can also be preserved by the desiccant method.

Narcissus

Cymbidium Orchid

Nymphaea

Nicandra

ORCHID This is a very large group of plants which, according to an old gardening book of mine, contains in the region of 15,000 species. Of these, the Cymbidium is one which in recent years has become familiar to us in the florist's shop, as it is used fairly extensively in wedding bouquets and corsages, and also as tourists to far-away places can never resist bringing some home as mementoes. It is for these reasons that I now include the Cymbidium orchid, for I feel it is a flower to preserve only for reasons of sentiment, not to include in a preserved arrangement for its decorative qualities.

PRESERVING The thick fleshy petals of the cream, pink or yellow flowers make it necessary to preserve it for three to four weeks using desiccant method No. 2, positioning. Although the flower's beautiful markings are retained, there is often a loss of much of its colour. Once preserved, the orchid's firm structure remains unchanged.

USES As a lasting keepsake, I would recommend making them into a picture, which should be glazed.

OX-EYE CHAMOMILE *see ANTHEMIS*

PAEONIA
PEONY There are thirty-three species of peony including hardy herbaceous and shrubby perennials (often referred to as tree peonies), flowering in late spring to early summer. I will make no attempt to describe all those suitable for preserving, but a few guidelines as to the flower forms with which I have had success, will, I feel, be helpful.

P. lutea ludlowii This is one of the shrubby peonies. It has single yellow flowers with dark stamens. This variety preserves particularly well because of the firm texture of its petals.
     Other shrubby peonies would also preserve well providing they have firm-textured petals. I have preserved one from a friend's garden, which has small rusty-red flowers which are most attractive.

P. officinalis
'Rubra-plena' I refer to this as the old cottage-garden herbaceous peony. Its large really double, almost globular crimson flower heads preserve exceptionally well, in fact I find it one of the most successful large garden flowers. The flowers tend to darken, which is common with this colour in all flowers, but if you use the protective spray described on page 151, its light-reflecting qualities will be improved, and when displayed under artificial light, its colour will be enhanced.
     Other double forms of peonies preserve well, but I find the pale shades tend to lose their colour. Herbaceous varieties with large single flowers preserve beautifully. However, due to their enormous size, even when the petals are treated with a protective spray, unless kept in absolutely dry conditions, they are inclined to collapse. I prefer to keep them in store and bring them out for special occasions. Out of season, these beautifully showy flowers, with their marvellous sculptured forms, will certainly impress your guests.

HARVESTING AND PRESERVING Single-flowered varieties should be gathered at a particularly open cup-shaped stage. Double varieties can be picked from the bud stage to fully open blooms, but take care not to pick any in which the seedpod is beginning to swell and protrude from the centre. At this stage the flower head will almost certainly fall apart during the process of preserving. Use desiccant method No. 2, positioning.

PHLOMIS
P. fruiticosa
JERUSALEM SAGE This is an evergreen shrub with heads of deep yellow florets produced in one, or often two, whorls. When the florets die, persistent green flower-like calyces remain which become firm and tough and are extremely decorative.

HARVESTING AND PRESERVING Can be gathered in full flower or after the flowers have withered and fallen out. Remove the leaves and use air method No. 1 or No. 2.

PHYSALIS
P. franchetii
CHINESE LANTERN
or **CAPE GOOSEBERRY** Also commonly known as winter cherry, this hardy perennial is in fact a native of Japan. Although it produces insignificant flowers, these are followed by large green inflated calyces which later turn bright orange-red.

HARVESTING AND PRESERVING Gather some when fully developed but still green, others as they turn yellow, and then finally collect the fully mature orange-red shades. This provides a selection of colours which you will find more interesting than simply relying on the orange-red with which we are all familiar. Preserve using air method No. 2. When dry remove the withered leaves. Lanterns which have been removed from their main stem can be laid on a tray to dry, after which they will need to be wired as shown on page 152. To make more decorative flower-like forms, use a small pair of sharp-pointed scissors to cut down each of the five ribs. The petal-like shapes can then be opened up to resemble a flower.

Paeonia
officinalis

Phlomis
fruiticosa

Paeonia
lutea ludlowii

A.

B.

Physalis
franchettii

Protea

PROTEA These South African shrubs, with colourful artichoke-like heads, are in fact the country's national flower. The protea is also an important commercial cut flower which is the reason I have included it in this section. For many years, species of protea have been imported into Britain in their dried brown state, but it is now possible to purchase fresh flower heads from florists, both here and in America. The species usually available have large heads which consist of large pinkish outer bracts, opening into a goblet shape, with smaller fringed inner bracts surrounding a hairy yellow flower boss, just like the artichoke. In some proteas this hairy fringe is dark brown, giving a striking contrast to the pink bracts.

PRESERVING In their fresh state all proteas can be dried by air method No. 2, but I have preserved some in a desiccant which I find keeps them in a more open position.

NOTE Due to their extremely firm texture, proteas can be enjoyed in their fresh state for a period of time before air drying or preserving to retain their colour.

ROSA
ROSE This is usually the one summer flower that everyone wants to preserve, not only because it is among the most widely grown of all garden flowers, but also due to its extensive use as a florist's flower in wedding bouquets, corsages, presentation arrangements and even that special gift of a single rose on St Valentine's Day. When dealing with roses for presentation, I feel it is more important to explain the forms of roses that preserve most successfully, rather than the species.
   1. Most florists' roses preserve remarkably well due to their firm compact habit of growth, but avoid those that are fully open with the stamens visible. Select instead blooms that are partially open with the centre petals still tightly closed, as illustrated.
   2. Choose garden varieties at the same stage of growth as florists' roses.
   3. Rambler roses, which belong to the group known as Wichuraiana ramblers, are ideal for preservation. These roses bloom profusely during June and July, bearing large trusses of small flowers. Varieties include 'Dorothy Perkins' (pink) and 'Alberic Barbier' (yellow buds opening white) which should be gathered while still at the yellow stage.
   4. Miniature roses are a must for miniature arrangements, and either buds or partially open flowers preserve well. Individual flowers of the rambler roses can also be used for this purpose.

HARVESTING AND PRESERVING Gather roses at the stages of growth suggested. Preserve using desiccant method No. 2, positioning, for individual flowers, and No. 4 for complete trusses of rambler roses.

SALIX
WILLOW There are many species of willow, both naturalised and grown under cultivation.
   The goat willow, *S. caprea,* is one of Britain's most beautiful native trees. The flowering catkins which appear on the leafless branches are gathered at Easter as 'palms', but to many people pussy willow is a more familiar name for this willow. *S. daphnoides,* a species which has beautifully soft furry silvery-grey catkins, is but one cultivated species which is also attractive.

HARVESTING AND PRESERVING If gathered shortly after the buds burst, and treated by glycerine method No. 1, short branches of catkins or 'pussies' will remain soft and supple and will develop a beautiful silken sheen. My reason for preserving pussy willow is to capture the catkins at this early stage of growth which I think is so attractive for use as a semi-permanent background for spring flowers.

SALVIA
SAGE The family of salvias is an exceptionally large one and includes our familiar culinary sage from the vegetable garden. Although this and many others produce long-lasting spikes of calyces, not all are sufficiently decorative or colourful to consider for preserving. There are also many with which I am not familiar. The following, therefore, represent but a few of the annuals, biennials and perennials which are available and preserve well.

S. horminum
CLARY Clary is a charming hardy annual which is grown only for its colourful leaf-like bracts, the flowers being small and inconspicuous. I have included it in the flower section, however, for, although leaf-like in form, the bracts have the bright colours usually found in flowers. In shades of rose, purple, purple-blue and white, these make a colourful summer display. Unfortunately seed catalogues so often list clary as being suitable just for hanging up to dry, the result of which is a lot of frustrated growers asking me why, after doing just that, they have all shrivelled up. As far as I am aware, although termed as a bract, the leafy bract of the clary remains soft like the leaves

Salix

A.

Rosa

B

Salvia norminum

Salvia splendens

Salvia superba

S. horminum
CLARY

of other bedding plants. For this reason, the only way in which it can be preserved is by using the desiccant method which results in a rather fragile structure.

NOTE Personally I prefer to enjoy clary for its beauty in the garden during the summer months and do not bother to preserve it.

S. splendens
SCARLET SAGE

This is one of the most familiar, and probably the most brilliant, of summer bedding plants. Although strictly speaking a perennial, it is today grown as an annual and provides a striking display of scarlet blooms from summer to early autumn. The reason for the apparently long-lasting blooms is because each scarlet flower is enveloped in an equally bright scarlet calyx from which it protrudes like a tongue. As the flowers fade, the calyces become firm and in time rather papery.

HARVESTING AND PRESERVING Leave them as long as possible before gathering. Actually it is not really necessary to spoil the bedding effect, but, when the beds are cleared, just cut the best stems before you relinquish the plants to the compost heap. Preserve by air method No. 3.

NOTE The flower spikes dry to a more subtle shade of red which I find very pleasing.

S. superba

As its name implies, this salvia produces particularly striking lavender-like flower spikes in which not only are the flowers and tiny bracts which surround them deep purple, but also the stems. Grown as a half-hardy annual this salvia will provide colourful flowering spikes, both in the garden and later for preserving. There are many other salvias, both annuals and perennials, which are similar to *S. superba* in both colour and form. No doubt these would preserve equally as well, although the flower spikes may not be quite so rich in colour.

HARVESTING AND PRESERVING Pick late in summer when the calyces are mature and firm. If the flowers are withered and look tatty, they can be carefully pulled out. Preserve by air method No. 1 or No. 3.

SANTOLINA
S. chamaecyparissus
COTTON LAVENDER

A hardy evergreen shrubby plant with silvery grey aromatic foliage which, in late summer, produces, according to the variety, small pale or deep yellow globular flower heads on long stiff wiry stems. These are ideal for small arrangements.

HARVESTING AND PRESERVING Gather flowers that are fully open but avoid any that are past maturity, at which stage they tend to lose their yellow colouring and turn brown. Preserve using air method No. 1 or No. 2.

SEA HOLLY

see ERYNGIUM

SEDUM
S. spectabile

These hardy perennial, autumn-flowering sedums, in spite of a certain amount of colour being lost, still remain attractive after preservation. Their large heads are similar in character to those of the achillea, and consist of many tiny star-like florets. Varieties include 'Autumn Joy', 'Meteor', and 'Ruby Red', which provide colours of rosy-pink, carmine-red or ruby-red.

HARVESTING AND PRESERVING Pick as the florets begin to open. Because of their succulent stems, they will continue to open during the process of preservation. Use air method No. 1 or No. 4.

SILENE
S. vulgaris
BLADDER CAMPION

Found growing wild throughout Britain and North America, the bladder campion is one of the large family of plants known as Caryophyllaceae. While all these plants have particularly decorative flower-like calyces, most are small and ideally suited only to miniature arrangements. The calyx of the bladder campion is larger and has a somewhat inflated appearance which makes it suitable for small arrangements.

HARVESTING AND PRESERVING The flower-like form of the calyces of any of these plants is only revealed after the petals of the flower have withered and fallen, at which time the calyx becomes firm and dry. To complete the drying process, use the air method No. 2. These green calyces will in time turn an attractive parchment colour.

SOLIDAGO
S. canadensis
GOLDEN ROD

Both the tall and dwarf varieties of this late-summer-flowering hardy perennial preserve equally well. Varieties include 'Crown of Rays' which is a mustard-yellow and 'Lemore', a soft primrose. The flower heads are in the form of a pyramidal panicle, each panicle consisting of masses of minute florets.

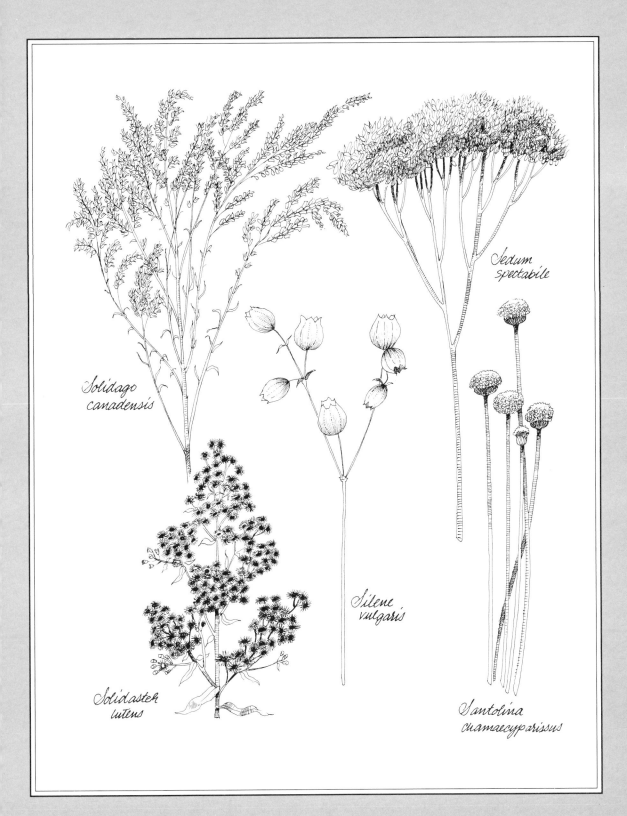

Solidago
canadensis

Sedum
spectabile

Silene
vulgaris

Solidaster
luteus

Santolina
chamaecyparissus

SOLIDAGO
S. canadensis
GOLDEN ROD

HARVESTING AND PRESERVING Gather before the florets are completely open. If left until fully open they have a tendency to become fluffy after preservation. Use air method No. 1 or No. 3.

USES Arrangements. For small arrangements each flower head can be divided into smaller sprays.

SOLIDASTER
S. lutens

This looks like a cross between a golden rod and a dwarf Michaelmas daisy. Although the florets on each head number less than on golden rod, in size each is in fact much larger and resembles a tiny daisy. This hardy perennial flowers in summer to early autumn.

HARVESTING AND PRESERVING Gather before the lower florets fade, regardless of whether or not the top florets are open. Use desiccant method No. 1 or No. 4, positioning, depending on the formation of each individual head.

USES Small or miniature arrangements.

SPIREA
S. arguta
BRIDAL WREATH

There are two shrubby spiraeas which are extremely decorative for preserved work.
This produces graceful arching sprays which are covered in tiny white flowers during April and early May.

S. van houttei

This produces its tiny white flowers, in clusters, at intervals along its stem, in early June.

HARVESTING AND PRESERVING Gather before the petals of the first flowers drop, which will mean preserving stems on which there are many unopened buds. Use desiccant method No. 4, positioning.

USES Complete stems of both spireas can be used for arrangements. Individual clusters of *S. van houttei* can be wired for miniature arrangements.

STACHYS
S. lanata
LAMB'S TONGUE

Apart from providing us with their lovely silvery leaves which are listed on page 72, this plant also produces tall spikes of rather uninteresting pinkish-mauve florets. However, each floret is enveloped in an attractive silvery flower-like calyx, and these calyces completely encircle the stem, covering at least three quarters of its length. Both the stems and the calyces have the same furry texture as the leaves and are extremely decorative.

SPECIAL NOTE There is a form called 'Silver Carpet' which, unfortunately, very rarely flowers.

HARVESTING AND PRESERVING Gather as the flowers mature and begin to fade, for it is at this stage that the spikes often begin to flop about and look rather untidy in the garden. However, even this has its advantages for it does mean that it is possible to gather some which have developed interesting shapes. The flowers can be preserved using air method No. 1, but will easily shatter unless carefully handled. I prefer to use glycerine method No. 2 to provide a more supple and therefore easier-to-handle stem. Pull out each tiny floret before or after preserving.

NOTE I find the stems are far more decorative when the florets have been pulled out.

SYRINGA
LILAC

A hardy deciduous shrub which flowers in late spring. Due to the closely packed florets on each stem, the single form retains its true character much better than the double. There are several shades of lilac-blue and mauve, but one of my favourites is 'Massena' which is a deep reddish-purple—the colour of which is well retained after preservation. There are several white forms which retain their colour well. I had hoped the variety called 'Primrose' would be more yellow, but when preserved it turns a rather attractive shade of cream.

HARVESTING AND PRESERVING Gather before the lower flowers begin to fade, when the flowers at the tip of each head will still be at the bud stage. With many of the larger heads I usually find it more satisfactory to divide them into smaller sections in the same way as I recommend for hydrangea, see Fig. 31, page 152. Preserve using the desiccant method No. 4.

TAGETES
MARIGOLD

There are several species of these half-hardy annuals, each with many varieties, but it is the double forms of the following varieties that I find most successful for preserving.

T. errecta

This is the African Marigold, some varieties of which bear flowers up to 10 cm (4 in) across, although, if possible, I like to select slightly smaller blooms. 'First Lady' is a good variety with bright clear-yellow double flowers which, having compact heads of tightly packed petals, retain their shape extremely well. Another good variety is 'Golden Age', with golden yellow flowers of similar form.

Stachys
lanata

Spirea
arguta

Tagetes
patula

Spirea
van houttei

Zinnia

Teucrium
scorodonia

T. patula   This is the dwarf French marigold which is a popular bedding plant. 'Boy-o-Boy' is a variety with tight double flowers in an attractive blend of colours—golden yellow, bright yellow, deep orange and mahogany red.

HARVESTING AND PRESERVING Gather the flowers as soon as they are fully open. With maturity, seeds begin to form within the calyx at the base of the petals, and if preserved at this stage, the petals are apt to become loose and drop out. Use desiccant method No. 2, positioning.

TANACETUM VULGARE   *see CHRYSANTHEMUM*

TANSY   *see CHRYSANTHEMUM VULGARE*

TEUCRIUM
T. scorodonia
WOODSAGE   Common throughout the British Isles in deciduous woodlands, rough grassland and on heathland, this wild plant is perhaps seldom noticed in its natural habitat, due to its colouring. It has spikes of tiny green flower-like calyces from which protrude insignificant yellow-green flowers. Studied closely, each calyx resembles a miniature lily of the valley floret.

HARVESTING AND PRESERVING Gather in September when the tiny flowers have faded, leaving the stems of persistent green calyces which, by now, will be mature and firm. Dry using air method No. 1. When dry remove the leaves and carefully pull out the dead flowers, leaving the stems of flower-like calyces. These look exquisite if the tips of the calyces are touched with a flick of white paint.

WATER LILY   *see NYMPHAEA*

WINDFLOWER   *see ANEMONE*

WOODSAGE   *see TEUCRIUM*

YARROW   *see ACHILLEA*

ZINNIA   The range of jewel-like shades in both the large-flowered varieties and the miniatures, combined with the firm texture of their overlapping petals make this summer-flowering half-hardy annual a must for preserved arrangements. Of the many strains listed in seed catalogues, with one exception, I think I can safely say that all are ideal for preservation. The exception is the chrysanthemum-flowered varieties.

HARVESTING AND PRESERVING It is important to gather only fully developed flowers, as flowers picked as they begin to open will not retain a good form when preserved. The stems are reasonably stiff, but I would advise reinforcing them with wire to prevent them from flopping over just below the calyx. Use desiccant method No. 2, positioning.

Annual everlasting flowers to grow from seed

Due to their characteristic texture or form, these flowers are usually collectively referred to as everlasting or immortelles. I have grouped them together in a separate section for easy reference, as they are all ideal for growing, both in the garden and on a wider commercial basis, primarily for the purpose of drying for decoration. Most of these flowers are natives of warmer climates—Australia, Africa, southern Europe and the Mediterranean regions. Therefore, in the British climate, in certain parts of the USA, or in fact anywhere in the northern hemisphere, they must be grown as hardy or half-hardy annuals.

Many people only know the word everlasting to mean bunches of helichrysums in mixed colours which can look rather crude and garish when grouped together. However, even these can be very effective if shades of one colour are selected and used in association with other flowers of a similar colouring, often providing the necessary brightness and depth of colour to an arrangement. Many of the other lesser-known everlastings differ enormously from each other, both in shape and form, and, like some of the new varieties of helichrysum, many are in the softer shades of pink and white.

GROWING, HARVESTING AND PRESERVING EVERLASTING FLOWERS

I have indicated its hardiness against each species, but details for sowing will be found both in seed catalogues and on seed packets. All species thrive in a light, well-drained soil in a sunny position.

Unless otherwise stated, the harvesting of these flowers should take place as soon as the blooms begin to open, as they will continue to open during the preserving process. Some everlastings have stems which remain firm and rigid when dry, but others will need to be wired as soon as they are gathered, unless of course you are making pictures or plaques, when only the heads will be used. Indication of wiring is given where necessary.

All the everlastings respond well to being dried by air method No. 1 (page 136). Due to their characteristic texture, there is no marked difference between dried and fresh flowers.

Helipterum
humboldtianum sandifosii

ACROCLINIUM
A. roseum
syn. **Helipterium roseum**

This half-hardy annual is a native of South-Western Australia. The name acroclinium is derived from the Greek words *akres*, top, and *kline*, a bed, apparently an indication of the shape of the open flowers.

Botanically, the acroclinium is now classed as helipterium, but as some seed catalogues still list it under its original name, I have done likewise as I feel its identification will thus be made easier, as it is so different in form from the true helipterium, as you will see. The pink daisy-like flowers are double, with either a yellow or black centre, and chaffy incurved petals of a soft texture. The stiff wiry stems make it an ideal flower for arrangements. Varieties of *Acroclinium roseum* include 'flore albo pleno', double white, and 'flore rosea pleno', double rose.

AMMOBIUM
A. alatum 'Grandiflorium'
SANDFLOWER

A native of Australia, in the USA this half-hardy annual is commonly called winged everlasting. The word ammobium (from the Greek words *ammos*, sand, and *bio*, to live), refers to the sandy soil in which the plant grows in its native habitat and also gives it its common name of sandflower. As the flowers open they reveal a domed yellow centre. This is surrounded by silvery-white bracts giving each flower the appearance of a dainty rosette. With maturity, the yellow centre turns brown and eventually falls out. Each stem can be successfully harvested while its many flowers are at various stages of growth, from tiny buds to fully developed blooms. The stiff stems of the ammobium make this an ideal flower for small arrangements, without the addition of false stems.

GLOBE AMARATH

see GOMPHRENA

GOMPHRENA
G. globosa
GLOBE AMARANTH

The name gomphrena is derived from the Greek word *gomphos*, meaning a club, which refers to the shape of the flowers. It is a tender half-hardy annual, which in appearance resembles a brilliant purple or pink clover flower. It may be necessary to replace the stem of this flower with a wire before preserving (see page 145).

HELICHRYSUM
H. bracteatum
STRAWFLOWER

Easily the best-known of the everlasting flowers, even during the Victorian era these half-hardy annuals were widely used in winter decorations. It is possibly for this reason, and also because of the rather harsh colouring of many, that today they are often despised. Grouped together in an arrangement, I find their colourings far from pleasing, but shades of one colour used with other flowers can be very effective. For example, the pinks and reds of *H. bracteatum* associate well with the pinks and reds of roses, zinnias and miniature dahlias, giving the brightness and depth of colour needed. Reference to a reputable seedsman's catalogue will show colours listed individually as well as mixed, which will enable you to grow only the colours required for your own personal needs. The colours include golden-yellow, salmon-rose, terracotta and shades of red including 'Hot Bikini', a really vibrant shade of yellow-red. There is also a creamy-white which is extremely useful.

HARVESTING Gather the main flower heads just as they are beginning to open. If these are required for arrangements, they will need wiring immediately, as shown on page 145. The buds on the side shoots can either be gathered at bud stage (ideal for miniature arrangements) or left to develop fully and gathered as previously mentioned.

HELIPTERUM
H. humboldtianum sandforii

The name helipterum is derived from the Greek words *helios*, the sun, and *pteron*, a wing. It is therefore not surprising that the flowered heads of this half-hardy annual are comprised of many tiny single star-like flowers of a rich golden yellow. These are ideal for plaques or pictures, but if used in arrangements, the stems will need strengthening.

H. manglesii, which bears rose-coloured flowers, and its white variety *alba*, see under its original name of rhodanthe.

H. roseum

For varieties 'flore albo pleno', double white, and 'flore roseo pleno', double rose, see under the original name of acroclinium.

Gomphrena
globosa

Acroclinium
roseum

Ammobium
alatum grandiflorum

Helichrysum
bracteatum

Helipterum
humboldtianum sandifosii

LIMONIUM
STATICE

There could be a little confusion over this group of half-hardy annuals which are sometimes classed as limonium and sometimes statice. There are both annuals and perennials. Some of these are natives of the British Isles and North America, while others come from warmer climates, but all have one thing in common: their suitability for drying by the air method.

L. dumosa

This is the pretty white branching statice which is sold by florists and makes a useful addition to small arrangements. Unlike *L. latifolium* and *L. vulgare*, it keeps its colour well.

L. latifolium

This is a beautiful hardy perennial, with branching heads of minute mauve flowers. Compared to *L. sinuatum*, it is very much daintier, but not so valuable as its colour soon fades to white.

L. sinuatum

By far the best-known are these half-hardy annuals which are commonly known to us, and are usually listed in seed catalogues, as statice. Their firm rigid branching stems of tiny funnel-shaped flowers, in shades of cerise, lavender, dark blue and yellow, have been used in winter decorations for years, and are marketed widely through florist's shops. Also available, but less common, are shades of apricot-pink and white. In arrangements I prefer to see these flowers used in the same way as the helichrysum, divided into colour groups using flowers of one colour at a time, either on their own or mixed with other flowers in shades of the same, or harmonising, colours. Seeds of individual colours packeted separately are obtainable, with varieties which include: 'Bondueii', yellow, 'Chamois Rose', apricot-pink and 'Market Growers' Blue', deep blue. Mixed colours are also available.

L. suworowii

Although a half-hardy annual, the flower heads of this statice differ considerably from other forms of limonium, being in the form of long dense spikes, sometimes growing erect, but often twisting into rather wonderful shapes as they reach maturity.

HARVESTING Wait until all the flowers are fully open before gathering varieties of statice for drying.

LONAS
L. indora
AFRICAN DAISY

In appearance this half-hardy annual is rather like a small form of achillea, as the golden yellow florets are borne in dense clusters forming flat heads. Having given this description of lonas many years ago, I have recently seen it actually called a small form of achillea, which of course it is not. Although the flower heads of lonas are much smaller than the achillea, individually each button-like floret is in fact much larger. The stems of this plant are firm and rigid, making the need for wiring unnecessary.

RHODANTHE
R.manglessii syn. **Helipterium manglessii**
SWAN RIVER EVERLASTING

Botanically like the acroclinium, this half-hardy annual is classed as helipterum. However I am still able to find it listed under its original name in some seed catalogues.

The daisy-like flowers, with yellow centres, are smaller than those of the acrolinium, and nodding. They have the same soft chaffy petals, although not so incurved, and, unlike the acroclinium, protrude from a mass of silvery bracts which cover the back of the flower like tiny scales.

Varieties are 'Maculata Alba', with small white flowers, and 'Rosea', a beautiful rose colour flushed with a darker shade of rose round its yellow centre. R. *manglessii* has bright rose, pink or white flowers.

SEA LAVENDER

see LIMONIUM

STATICE

see LIMONIUM

XERANTHEMUM (H.A.)

This hardy annual is a native of southern Europe. The name xeranthemum is derived from the Greek word *xeros*, meaning dry, referring to the dry papery texture of the daisy-like heads.

Usually available in shades of rose, pink and purple, its petals are longer and rather more spike-like than most other everlasting flowers. The stems are stiff and wiry.

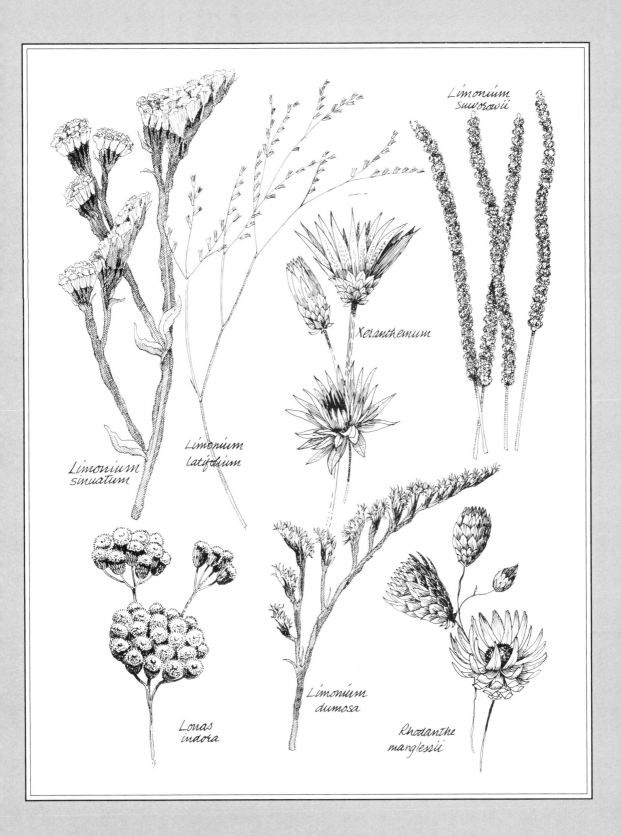

Limonium
suworowii

Xeranthemum

Limonium
latifolium

Limonium
sinuatum

Limonium
dumosa

Lonas
indora

Rhodanthe
manglessii

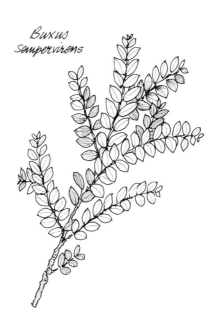

Buxus
sempervirens

2 FOLIAGE

Whatever type of preserved work is undertaken, it is inevitable that foliage in some form or other will be needed. For preserved flower arrangements, foliage provides the necessary backbone, just as it does in fresh flower arrangements. So often I have seen dried arrangements overstuffed with flowers in an attempt to cover the mechanics, without so much as a leaf in sight. To recreate a typical Victorian posy arrangement, with the emphasis on flowers, can look quite charming, but, generally speaking, with fresh flower arranging having reached such a high standard, I am surprised how often dried or preserved arrangements fail to reach this standard because of the total absence of foliage of any kind whatsoever.

During winter a small collection of preserved foliage can be extremely useful when fresh deciduous foliage is unobtainable and fresh evergreen foliage may be in limited supply or difficult to pick due to adverse weather conditions. At this time of year even the most dedicated gardener will often succumb to a small bunch of florist's chrysanthemums for which a background of preserved foliage will be invaluable. This aspect, of using preserved foliage with fresh flowers, offers tremendous scope. Although this book deals only with natural dried and preserved plant materials, and not artificial ones, there are nevertheless occasions when the use of artificial flowers may be appropriate. In particular I am thinking of silk flowers, some of which are extremely well made and often bear a remarkably true likeness to their real counterparts, both in colour and form, although, when arranged on their own, even these can seldom deceive the eye into thinking they are real. But when these same flowers are arranged against a background of preserved foliage, the eye immediately notices that the foliage is real and often accepts the flowers without question.

From the range of trees and shrubs to be found in the countryside or in the average garden, it is possible to preserve a wide selection of foliage which, as the illustrations show, will provide the arranger with a great diversity of leaf shapes and forms, and also an extended range of colours, quite often from what was originally just plain green foliage. With many of the bold evergreen leaf forms, such as fatsia or mahonia, as few as three leaves are often sufficient for the centre of an arrangement, with the addition of a few branches of smaller-leaved foliage for the outline. Here of course I have been referring to foliage which is preserved by the glycerine method, as described on page 139, this being the generally accepted way of preserving foliage for arrangements, enabling it to retain its pliable texture. There are, however, many other leaves which can be preserved, although not in this way. They include the silver leaves, and green leaves with interesting markings or varigated colour, and also the beautiful red and yellow leaves of autumn. I have found that all of these can be preserved by the desiccant method in the same way as described for flowers (see page 145).

Although I have given illustrated details of the foliage which I have found to preserve well, I hope these will also serve as a guide for the arranger when needing to select other foliage of similar form and texture.

ACAENA
A. buchanani
NEW ZEALAND BURR

This is a hardy evergreen (or perhaps I should say evergrey) rock plant of creeping habit, with tiny, very attractive finely divided leaves of a beautiful grey green or silver green. In late autumn I find many of the leaves turn a beautiful salmon-pink.

A. microphylla

Of the same form and habit of growth as *buchananii*, but with lovely bronze leaves.

HARVESTING AND PRESERVING Gather at any time during summer and autumn, or the early part of the winter. Preserve both species using the desiccant method. An ideal foliage for miniatures but requiring careful handling.

ALCHEMILLA
A. mollis
LADY'S MANTLE

This hardy herbaceous plant is mainly valued for its flowers (see page 12). Its leaves, too, are well worth preserving due to their attractive shape. They have a hairy, almost velvet-like, texture.

HARVESTING AND PRESERVING Fully mature leaves should be gathered from late summer through autumn. Preserve using glycerine method No. 2. They can also be preserved by the desiccant method.

ALEXANDRIAN LAUREL

see DANAE RACEMOSA

ARBUTUS
A. unedo
STRAWBERRY TREE

This large evergreen bush, or small tree, has branches of dark shiny green leathery leaves which are compact in their habit of growth, making them particularly suitable for preserving.

HARVESTING AND PRESERVING Cut when all the leaves on the branch are fully mature. Usually late summer, through autumn to winter is the best time. Preserve using glycerine method No. 1.

ASPIDISTRA

A favourite evergreen house plant of the Victorian era, this was commonly called the parlour palm. In recent years, with the increasing popularity of house plants enjoying a welcome revival, the aspidistra has become much sought after, especially among flower arrangers, due to the rather unique form of its long tough broad leaves.

HARVESTING AND PRESERVING Gather mature leaves and preserve by glycerine method No. 2.

AUCUBA
A. japonica
SPOTTED LAUREL

A distinctive dense, evergreen laurel-like shrub but with leaves which I feel have a more elegant appearance, being less solid-looking than those of the laurel.

HARVESTING AND PRESERVING Gather short branches of mature leaves and preserve them using glycerine method No. 1. The result will be rich dark, almost black, foliage with the stems also developing the same colouring. It is extremely useful as it contrasts so well with the brighter shades of red and yellow flowers to make a striking arrangement. Use the special aftercare treatment described on page 140.

BARRENWORT

see EPIMEDIUM

BEECH

see FAGUS SYLVATICA

BETULA
BIRCH

A group of deciduous trees of which the silver birch, *Betula pendula*, is probably the best known. This tree provides graceful branches of foliage which I find particularly suitable for smaller arrangements because of the extremely dainty leaf formation.

HARVESTING AND PRESERVING Gather from July onwards while the foliage is still green, although I find, towards autumn, the leaves become damaged by insects. It is a matter of preference as to whether the catkins are removed or left on. Preserve using glycerine method No. 1.

BIRCH

see BETULA

BOX

see BUXUS

BROOM

see CYTISUS SCOPARIUS

BUTCHER'S BROOM

see RUSCUS

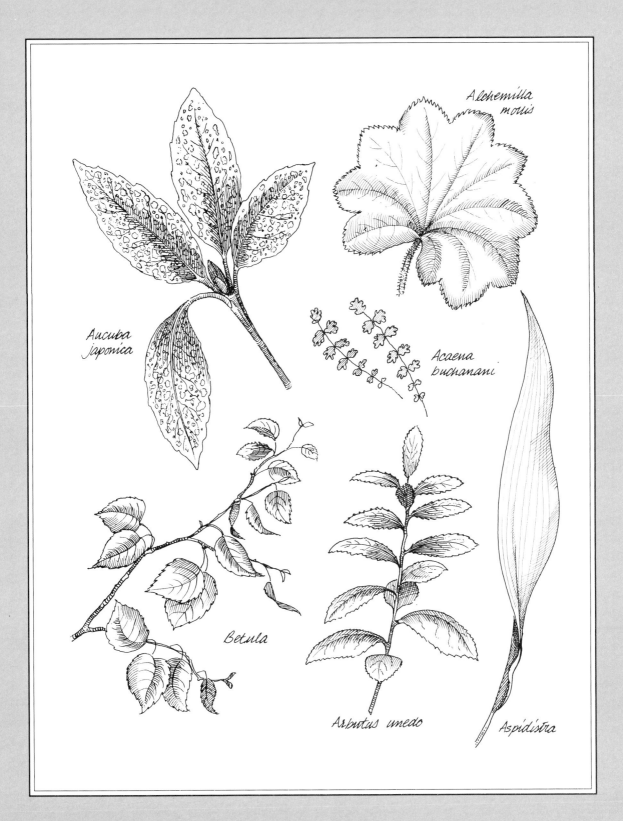

Alchemilla
mollis

Aucuba
japonica

Acaena
buchanani

Betula

Arbutus unedo

Aspidistra

BUXUS
B. sempervirens
COMMON BOX

An evergreen shrub or small tree with dense small glossy dark green leathery leaves.

HARVESTING AND PRESERVING Pick in late summer through autumn and winter. Preserve using glycerine method No. 1. After preserving this foliage will develop an almost golden shade which is extremely attractive.

CAMELLIA

This is an evergreen shrub or small tree with medium-sized tough glossy evergreen leaves, not unlike the texture of laurel but smaller and more attractive.

HARVESTING AND PRESERVING Gather in late summer through autumn and winter. Preserve using glycerine method No. 1, which will produce dark brown indestructable foliage useful for all types of preserved work. Use the special aftercare treatment described on page 140.

CASTANEA
C. sativa
SWEET CHESTNUT

This massive deciduous tree is grown for its edible nuts. Its elongated serrated leaves provide an interesting form for the preserved-flower arranger.

HARVESTING AND PRESERVING Gather short branches from July onwards while the leaves remain green. Preserve using glycerine method No. 1. After preserving, the leaves will often become floppy at the leaf joint, but I find this of little concern as they are far more useful when used individually with the addition of a false wire stem. Shades of dark olive green are usual as a result of preserving, although they later tend to turn brown.

CHERRY LAUREL

see PRUNUS LAUROCERASUS

CHOISYA
C. ternata
MEXICAN ORANGE BLOSSOM

In late spring and early summer the sweetly scented white flowers of this beautiful medium-size rounded bush are a joy, but it is the evergreen foliage for which choisya is invaluable to the flower arranger.

HARVESTING AND PRESERVING Pick at almost any time, but you will be most successful during summer and autumn. Cut branches of up to 30 cm (1 ft) and preserve them using glycerine method No. 1. For small arrangements, the attractive leaves can be removed from the main branch after preserving and wired individually. This is a particularly useful way of using this and other foliage which has become limp during preserving, which happens if the stems of the individual leaves are not fully mature.

CHRYSANTHEMUM
C. haradjanii

A perennial plant growing from 15–20 cm (6–8 in) high and of mat-forming habit, its sub-shrubby branches are covered with exquisite silvery grey, finely divided leaves, each resembling a tiny fern or feather. These are ideal for miniature arrangements.

HARVESTING AND PRESERVING Gather individual leaves at any stage, although the true characteristic fern-like appearance will only be found in leaves that are fully mature. Be sure to gather a selection of sizes; the smallest leaves can measure as little as 1 cm ($\frac{1}{2}$ in) in length. Preserve using the desiccant method. Careful handling is required after preservation, but these beautiful leaves are well worth the extra care needed.

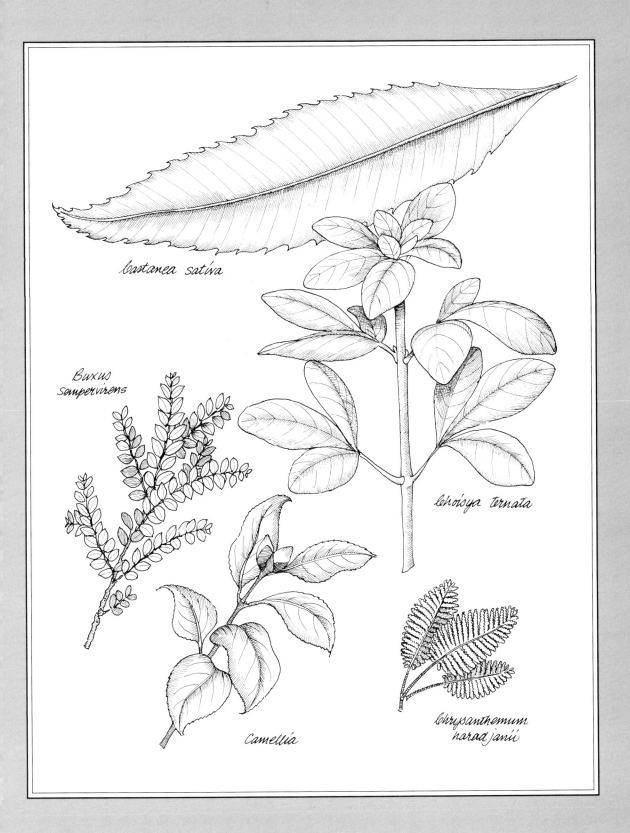

castanea sativa

Buxus
sempervirens

Choisya ternata

Camellia

Chrysanthemum
naradjanii

CINERARIA
C. maritima
syn. **Senecio cineraria**

Commonly called sea ragwort, or in the USA better known as dusty miller, this is usually treated as a half-hardy annual bedding plant, but I have found that it will survive the winter in Britain in a sheltered place. This plant is valuable for its beautifully cut silver leaves which vary from 5–15 cm (2–6 in) long. It is ideal for small arrangements.

HARVESTING AND PRESERVING Gather tiny immature or fully mature leaves depending on requirements. The immature leaves are suitable for miniature arrangements. Preserve using the desiccant method.

COMMON BOX

see BUXUS SEMPERVIRENS

COTONEASTER

There are many, both evergreen and deciduous, cotoneasters which are useful for preserving, but I have chosen to describe the following as being particularly striking and differing considerably from each other in form.

C. franchetii

A tall semi-evergreen shrub with graceful branches of sage-green leaves with grey undersides.

HARVESTING AND PRESERVING The ideal time to gather is early summer at which time the clusters of tiny flowers will be retained. Gathered at this time or later, this foliage can be preserved by glycerine method No. 1. The upper surface of the leaves will turn brown, but the undersides will retain their grey colouring. This enables the foliage to be used either way, depending on the colouring of your arrangement and the desired effect.

C. horizontalis

This is a deciduous shrub with spreading branches, each growing in the form of a herringbone pattern. Not so useful as *C. franchetii*, its characteristic form can be a valuable asset when an unusual foliage formation is required.

HARVESTING AND PRESERVING The ideal time to gather is July–August, before the berries mature and dominate the branches. I feel it is more attractive for preserving without the berries, which turn brown and shrivel. Preserve using glycerine method No. 1.

CRATAEGUS
C. monogyna
HAWTHORN

Widely planted in Britain as a field or roadside hedge, *Crataegus monogyna* is the common deciduous hawthorn. I remember as a child that local villagers called it may, obviously because this is the month in which it flowers. There are also many other species which grow throughout Europe. This is a foliage which I seldom see used in flower arrangements (perhaps because in many country areas it is considered unlucky to bring it indoors), although it is extremely attractive and dainty in spite of the thorns which are by no means excessive.

HARVESTING AND PRESERVING Gather at any time from July till autumn and preserve by glycerine method No. 1. This foliage turns dark green within a few days and retains this colouring for many months before going brown.

cotoneaster
franchetii

cineraria
maritima

cotoneaster
horizontalis

crataegus
monogyna

CROCOSMIA
MONTBRETIA

There are many forms of this late-summer-flowering herbaceous montbretia, all producing long strap-like leaves which are invaluable for providing pointed plant material for an arrangement. The leaves of the most common, almost wild, variety are quite slender, while those of the other forms are broader and conspicuously ribbed with an unusual pleated effect.

HARVESTING AND PRESERVING Use glycerine method No. 2, allowing not more than one week to process. These leaves will darken, but only slightly, and will remain green for many months. The narrow leaves eventually turn a biscuit colour, while the wider ones will usually turn brown.

CUPRESSUS

In British gardens we grow many varieties of cupressus, all of which are evergreen. Some forms are used as hedging shrubs, others as specimen trees. Apart from the common green shades, many have bright yellow foliage, while others are a beautiful glaucous blue.

HARVESTING AND PRESERVING Picked in July and August the varieties with yellow and glaucous blue foliage are at their best, their colouring producing its most intense hue which will be retained for many months if preserved by the air method. I find the ease of preserving large quantities of foliage in this way ensures plenty of foliage for filling in an arrangement. Careful handling will be necessary as it is somewhat brittle.

NOTE It is the formation and texture of this foliage (having no proper leaf form) that enables it to be preserved by this method without shrivelling. As an alternative, glycerine method No. 1 can be used. Preserved in this way the foliage will retain its pliable and supple quality, but will darken in colour and eventually turn brown.

CYTISUS
C. scoparius
COMMON BROOM

The well-known common broom is found throughout Europe except in the north. There are also many cultivated forms available. It is valuable not for its leaf-covered branches, but for the graceful branches themselves.

HARVESTING AND PRESERVING Pick at any time of year when weather conditions permit. Preserve using glycerine method No. 1. Broom can also be encouraged to develop wonderful curves by bending and tying it in the desired shape and then allowing it to dry naturally before untying.

DANAE
D. racemosa
ALEXANDRIAN LAUREL

A charming evergreen shrub, or maybe more accurately a shrub-like plant, its leaf formation and habit of growth is like that of butcher's broom of which it is a close relative, although unlike the erect stiff stems and leaves produced by butcher's broom, *Danae racemosa* produces long graceful arching sprays of leaves which are soft and pliable and exceptionally glossy.

HARVESTING AND PRESERVING The new foliage produced from ground level each year will preserve by glycerine method No. 1 equally as well as the more mature foliage. It will also preserve to a much paler shade than foliage preserved later in the season. Weather conditions permitting, I have been able to preserve perfect undamaged stems of this foliage in midwinter.

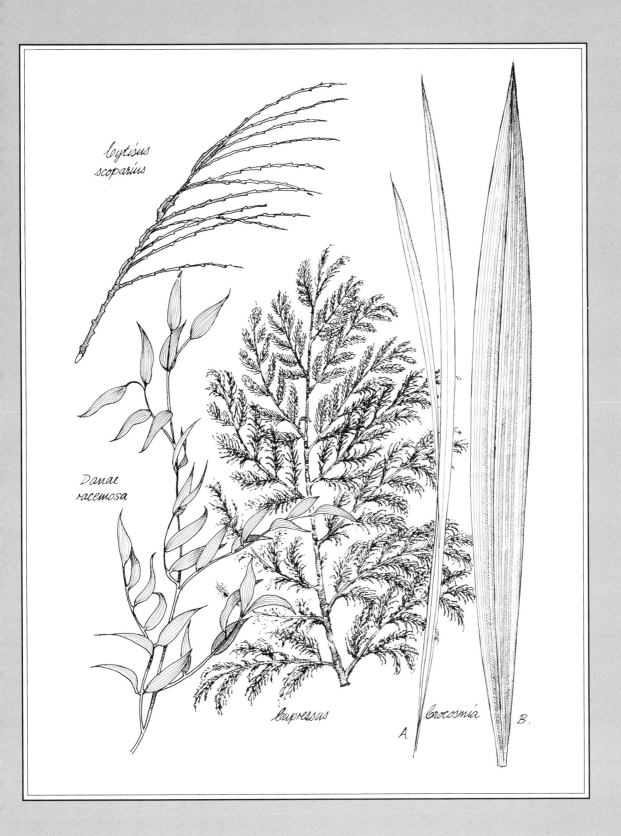

Cytisus
scoparius

Danae
racemosa

Cupressus

Crocosmia

A.

B.

ECHINOPS
GLOBE THISTLE

The spiky steel-blue globular flower of the echinops are well known to the flower arranger and are fully described on page 26, but the leaves of this thistle-like plant may often be overlooked for it is their beautiful silvery undersides which are so attractive and particularly welcome as one of the few silvery leaves for preserved arrangements. Their shape, too, is of particular interest.

HARVESTING AND PRESERVING Gather mature leaves of all sizes and preserve by the desiccant method.

ELAEAGNUS
E. pungens 'Maculata'

This is an evergreen shrub with smooth medium-sized golden yellow leaves with a green margin. It is valuable when golden foliage is required, for although the leaves retain their green margin for many months, it eventually fades, but the leaves retain their golden colour indefinitely.

HARVESTING AND PRESERVING Cut from September onwards throughout the winter. If picked earlier, many immature leaves lack the intense gold colouring and have a somewhat rough, rather than the smooth and shiny, surface which is a characteristic feature of the 'Maculata'. Preserve using glycerine method No. 1.

NOTE I find individual leaves wired into sprays are particularly useful (see page 154).

E. × ebbingei

This is a hybrid of *E. macrophylla* × *E. pungens*. It is a very fast-growing evergreen shrub, and its green leaves have a distinctive silvery underside. I think its habit of growth is more graceful than 'Maculata' which provides far more useful sprays of foliage for preserving.

HARVESTING AND PRESERVING Gather mature foliage and preserve using glycerine method No. 1. If picked complete with its inconspicuous silvery flowers, these, together with the undersides of the leaves, will remain silver. The green upper surface of the leaves will eventually turn a pale sherry colour which I find most pleasing.

EPIMEDIUM
BARRENWORT

There are several varieties of this herbaceous plant all of which have smooth heart-shaped leaves which taper to a point and grow in the form of a spray on a branched stem. Mature leaves have a remarkably firm texture and their stems are also very wiry, making this herbaceous plant particularly suitable for preserving.

HARVESTING AND PRESERVING Although often referred to as an evergreen, it cannot be considered as such from a preservation point of view. Glycerine method No. 2 is only effective for mature foliage picked from mid-summer till autumn. Although the leaves remain on the plant during the winter, they are actually in an almost dry state and, from autumn onwards, they must be preserved by the desiccant method.

Elaeagnus pungens 'maculata'

Elaeagnus x ebbingei

Epimedium

Echinops

ESCALLONIA This evergreen shrub is particularly common in British seaside gardens. I prefer to use the small-leaved hybrids for preserving, such as 'Peach Blossom'.

HARVESTING AND PRESERVING It is possible to preserve quite long sprays providing these shrubs are not used as hedging and constantly being trimmed. Preserve using glycerine method No. 1. The leaves turn almost black after only four to five days in the mixture, and for this reason I find preserved escallonia useful as a striking contrast to brighter flowers. Its long sprays are also particularly suitable to outline an arrangement.

EUCALYPTUS
GUM TREE The gum trees are natives of Australia and Tasmania and for this reason most are not hardy enough for general cultivation in the British Isles. However *E. gunnii* is one of the few which are reasonably hardy and, in sheltered areas, it can grow to a full-size tree of some 9–12 m (30–40 ft) or more. When the tree is young, it produces attractive grey, almost pewter-colour, disc-shaped leaves which, with maturity, become quite elongated. I like to keep my eucalyptus cut to more or less a bush to give me a constant supply of my favourite juvenile leaves. Other imported species of eucalyptus can be purchased from florists for preserving.

HARVESTING AND PRESERVING Preserve using glycerine method No. 1. Results will vary from a mauvish bronze shade in the younger leaves to a darkish shade of grey, with blue undertones, in the leaves of the mature tree. As the eucalyptus retains its leaves during the winter, foliage can be gathered at almost any time.

EUPHORBIA
E. robbiae
SPURGE Although grown and loved for its yellowish-green bracted flowers, these are produced from dark green rosettes of leathery evergreen leaves which preserve exceptionally well.

HARVESTING AND PRESERVING Gather stems of complete rosettes when the leaves are firm and mature, usually from midsummer onwards. Preserve using glycerine method No. 2. If after preserving the rosette shows signs of flopping open, turn it upside down and bind with a wire. This will ensure that a tight rosette form is retained.

Eucalyptus
species

Eucalyptus
gunnii

Euphorbia
robbiae

Escallonia

Eucalyptus
species

FAGUS
F. sylvatica
COMMON BEECH

This is possibly the most commonly preserved foliage and needs little description. I find the foliage from different beech trees can vary tremendously, both in size and shade of green, and for this reason alone there will be variations in the colour of the foliage in its preserved state.

HARVESTING AND PRESERVING Pick at any time from July onwards while the leaves remain green. The results of foliage preserved earlier rather than later in the season will also vary considerably. Preserve using glycerine method No. 1.

FATSIA
F. japonica

This is an evergreen shrub, the leaves of which are valuable for their quite distinctive architectural quality.

HARVESTING AND PRESERVING Due to their size, these leaves are preserved and used individually. The surface of each leaf is firm and glossy. The leaf also has quite a reasonable stalk, enabling it to be preserved by glycerine method No. 2.

NOTE Failure in successful preservation of these leaves is usually due to them collapsing at the neck. Details of how to avoid this are shown on page 141. Use also the special aftercare treatment described on page 140.

× **FATSHEDERA**

Described as a bigeneric hybrid between *Fatsia japonica* and *Hedera helix* 'Hibernica', this evergreen shrub is also used as a house plant. From the illustration it is easy to see the resemblance to its parent plants, but in size many of its large leaves are equivalent to those of *Fatsia japonica*.

HARVESTING AND PRESERVING Although these leaves do not have such a firm texture as fatsia, they do seem to preserve remarkably well (see fatsia for details).

GARRYA
G. elliptica

This is a graceful winter-flowering evergreen shrub or small tree with tough leathery leaves. The outstanding decorative value of its pendulous flowering catkins makes it a firm favourite of mine (see page 28). As an evergreen it is effective throughout the year, but the quality of its foliage is far superior if the shrub is grown in a sheltered place.

HARVESTING AND PRESERVING This foliage preserves most successfully from late summer through autumn, and, of course, during the winter catkin-flowering period. Use glycerine method No. 1.

GAULTHERIA
G. shallon

This lime-hating evergreen shrub is a native of western North America. It is just one of many species of gaultheria but the only one I know of which is suitable for preserving. It is a densely branched shrub with dark leathery leaves.

HARVESTING AND PRESERVING Gather from late summer through autumn and winter, weather permitting. Preserve using glycerine method No. 1.

GLOBE THISTLE   *see ECHINOPS*

Achillea and hydrangea flowers arranged against a background of hawthorn, oak, beech and hellebore foliage. At the centre of this pedestal arrangement, the hollyhock flowers with their distinct 'faces' provide a contrast to the more solid flower forms.

The rich colouring of dahlias, lilies and fremontia flowers blend well with the sprays of lime fruits, grasses and dock seedheads. Their colours are enriched by the dark rhododendron foliage. Empty iris seedcases provide an interesting feature in this arrangement.

To create this colourful arrangement in winter, dahlias, roses, delphiniums, statice and gypsophila were preserved and carefully stored, together with golden *Cupressus* and the individual leaves of Soloman's Seal. The colouring of this foliage provides a link with the lace-draped figurine.

Pinky-red hydrangea, deep red *Sedum*, silvery-bracted flowers of *Eryngium*, dock and *Rhus* seedheads, go well with soft furry *Stachys lanata*, delphinium seedheads and striped seedspikes of *Acanthus*. Individual leaves of Soloman's Seal and *Viburnum rhytidophyllum* used with their undersides uppermost harmonise with this colour scheme.

This arrangement of autumn foliage, dahlias and hydrangea with *Hosta* and montbretia leaves gives a welcome sunny glow to any room during the dull days of winter.

Featuring the large crimson flowers of *Paeonia officinalis* 'Rubra-plena' and *Mahonia japonica* berries. The steel blue hydrangeas were chosen to blend with the colouring of the berries. *Cupressus* and eucalyptus foliage was used sparingly in this somewhat unusual colour scheme.

A simple yet effective arrangement of wild grasses which were chosen for their contrasting forms. The subtly coloured wine bottle provides a simple but ideal container.

The large creamy bosses of the cardoon thistle together with glycerined pampas grasses are shown to advantage against a background of *Mahonia japonica* and beech foliage. Faded *Echinops* heads prove that any old plant material, provided it is in good condition, can be useful.

An outline of the beautiful sculptured forms of *Mahonia japonica, Fatsia* and oak leaves are used in this arrangement with just seven dahlias. The semi-permanent background of foliage would also be ideal to use for a few fresh flowers, particularly during the winter months.

Ballota, Alchemilla, dahlias, *Helichrysum*, hollyhocks and fever few, with desiccant-preserved sycamore leaves, are used here to create an arrangement of elegance and charm.

Two beautiful architectural forms of reconstructed *Acanthus* flowers with just two *Fatsia* leaves.

An interesting piece of tree root screwed to a natural wood base and covered with moss provides the perfect setting for an arrangement of *Helleborus niger* and heather with ivy leaves and ferns.

Fungi and ferns arranged in a natural setting of moss on a base of wood which still has the bark intact. The bracket fungi which are stuck in position appear to grow from the piece of pinewood, which has been completely sculptured by Nature. A simple grouping of daisies are the only flowers used.

This arrangement, which measures only fourteen inches in height, illustrates how dried and preserved white flowers which have a tendency to turn cream can make a charming arrangement, provided the use of a pure white container is avoided. The only foliage used was *Tellima* and box. The use of foliage was restrained to retain the overall cream effect.

A sundae glass holds a colourful arrangement of small air-dried flowers. *Achillea, Xeranthemum*, ammobium and *Santolina*, with desiccant-preserved *Hosta* and ivy leaves.

A basket measuring only ten inches in length filled with summer flowers, including rambler roses, *Alchemilla*, statice, *Dianthus* and *Santolina*, arranged with silver-grey *Cineraria* leaves.

Fagus sylvatica

Fatsia japonica

Garrya elliptica

X *Fatshedera*

GREVILLEA
SILK BARK OAK

This half-hardy shrub from Australia needs very mild conditions to survive in the British garden, and for this reason it is grown as an indoor or greenhouse foliage plant. Its attractive finely divided fern-like foliage makes it extremely useful for small arrangements, while divided into smaller segments, it is ideal for miniature arrangements.

HARVESTING AND PRESERVING Preserve mature leaves by glycerine method No. 2.

GUM TREE *see EUCALYPTUS*

HAWTHORN *see CRATAEGUS MONOGYNA*

HEDERA
IVY

The ivy needs no description. Primarily it is a foliage for the fresh-flower arranger, particularly in its many variegated forms, but some forms can also provide useful foliage to preserve. Here I refer to my own personal preferences which are the common wild ivy which, when found growing away from its main support, produces useful branches of shiny evergreen leaves. Trails of wild clinging ivy can produce beautiful bronze leaves with distinctive veining, particularly during winter months.

HARVESTING AND PRESERVING The short, somewhat dumpy, branches of wild green ivy preserve well by glycerine method No. 1. Trails of clinging wild ivy should be preserved using the desiccant method. Individual leaves of the small-leaved cultivated ivies can also be preserved by this method and are ideal for miniature arrangements.

HELLEBORE *see HELLEBORUS*

HELLEBORUS
H. foetidus
HELLEBORE

This is the native evergreen hellebore. Although now rarely found in the wild, it is commonly cultivated in gardens. Its large clusters of pendulous bell-shaped limey-green flowers are particularly attractive from January to April. On dull winter days, at a time when blooms in the garden are few, the flowers look particularly striking against the extremely dark green foliage, and the evergreen foliage is attractive all the year round. These plants readily seed and are very prolific on a chalky soil.

HARVESTING AND PRESERVING Gather fully mature leaves at any time of year and preserve using glycerine method No. 2, combined with the special treatment shown on page 141 to prevent the leaf flopping at its neck and therefore failing to absorb the glycerine mixture. The leaves of other forms of hellebore preserve equally well. *H. orientalis*, for example, is good, but I feel none are as good a shape as *H. foetidus*. The leaves of hellebores are particularly valuable for preserving as they provide a contrast to the many round and oval forms of other leaves. They respond well to the special aftercare treatment described on page 140.

HOSTA

Hostas are well known to the flower arranger for their decorative leaves, many of which have striking variegations. I feel it is not necessary to list them, but it is sufficient to say that it is possible to preserve them all.

HARVESTING AND PRESERVING Gather fully mature leaves which are firm and free from holes (slugs love them). *H. sieboldiana,* with its blue-green leaves, and other varieties with particularly tough leaves will respond to glycerine method No. 2, combined with the special treatment shown on page 141. Other less sturdy forms, such as *H. undulata,* with its green and cream variegated leaves, preserve well by the desiccant method which retains the colour and variegation for which these leaves are so prized. One word of warning—they will become rather brittle, but, if handled with care, and if possible treated with a special spray (see page 151), they will last for a very long time.

IVY *see HEDERA*

LADY'S MANTLE *see ALCHEMILLA*

LAMB'S EARS
or LAMB'S TONGUE *see STACHYS*

Helleborus foetidus

Grevillea

Hosta undulata

A.

Hedera

B

MAGNOLIA
M. grandiflora
BULL BAY

This is one of a large family of trees and shrubs from North America. Many are deciduous but the most suitable foliage for preserving is produced by *M. grandiflora* which is evergreen. This species is widely grown as an ornamental tree and produces large smooth green leaves which are laurel-like, only much larger. These are remarkably tough and, when preserved, are practically indestructable.

HARVESTING AND PRESERVING Gather short branches of fully mature leaves at any time of the year. Preserve using glycerine method No. 1. These will eventually turn a rich dark brown, but they do take several weeks to preserve. Afterwards, use the special grooming treatment described on page 140. Due to the extremely tough texture of these leaves, it is possible to gather mature fallen leaves and use them immediately with no further treatment. A wide range of golden brown shades will be found if you search carefully. Use the special aftercare treatment described on page 140.

MAHONIA
M. aquifolium
OREGON GRAPE

Although less spectacular than *M. japonica*, this evergreen shrub provides very useful foliage for preserving. The leaves are much smaller than *M. japonica* and 'Charity' often measuring less than half their length and of a less leathery texture. This makes them particularly suitable for smaller arrangements where a distinctive leaf form is required.

M. japonica

The large pinnate leaves of this handsome evergreen shrub have a tough leathery texture. In length they vary considerably, sometimes measuring 30 cm (1 ft) or even more. I consider they provide one of the most spectacular and valuable forms of foliage for preservation. Similar and equally suitable for preservation is 'Charity'.

HARVESTING AND PRESERVING Preserve using glycerine method No. 1. For *M. japonica* and 'Charity', allow three to four weeks; for *M. aquifolium*, about half this length of time. The leaves will turn a dark olive green, becoming brown after a year or more.

NOTE due to the extremely tough texture of *M. japonica* and 'Charity', leaves removed when only partially preserved will provide interesting variations of colour. It is essential to use the special aftercare treatment described on page 140.

MEXICAN ORANGE BLOSSOM *see CHOISYA*

MONTBRETIA *see CROCOSMIA*

NEW ZEALAND BURR *see ACAENA*

OAK *see QUERCUS*

OREGON GRAPE *see MAHONIA AQUIFOLIUM*

PAEONIA
PEONY

Many of the hardy perennial herbaceous peonies can provide us with beautifully sculptured leaf forms, particularly the shrubby peonies, which are often referred to as tree peonies. The foliage of these is more finely cut and when mature has a somewhat firmer texture.

HARVESTING AND PRESERVING Do not attempt to gather peony foliage for preserving until it is completely mature. From July onwards it will be sufficiently firm to obtain successful results by using the glycerine method. If each leaf is devided into smaller sections, these can be preserved using the desiccant method. After preserving each piece will need wiring, see page 153.

POLYGONATUM
P. multiflorum
SOLOMAN'S SEAL

This herbaceous plant produces long oval-shaped leaves spaced evenly along its tall arching stems.

HARVESTING AND PRESERVING Gather complete stems from mid to late summer when the leaves are fully mature and firm. Preserve using glycerine method No. 2. They will turn a lovely limey-green. If the leaves on the top of each stem are still immature, they will become very soft when preserved. I usually prefer to pinch these out, either before or after preserving.

NOTE I find that leaves removed from the stem and wired individually, as described on page 146, are extremely useful, a single stem often providing enough leaves for one small arrangement.

PRUNUS
P. laurocerasus
CHERRY LAUREL

This is the species of laurel most commonly grown; in fact in many areas it has become naturalized. It forms a large shrub or small tree. When preserved, its tough leathery leaves are an invaluable source of bold foliage for both preserved arrangements and as a foil for fresh flowers. Being smaller in size than the leaves of the magnolia they are generally more useful.

HARVESTING AND PRESERVING Gather short branches of mature leaves from early autumn through till spring. Preserve using glycerine method No. 1 which will result in dark brown leaves which are not only the texture, but the colour, of leather and will last indefinitely. I find the laurel-leaf sprays more useful if divided up after preserving and wired individually (see page 153).

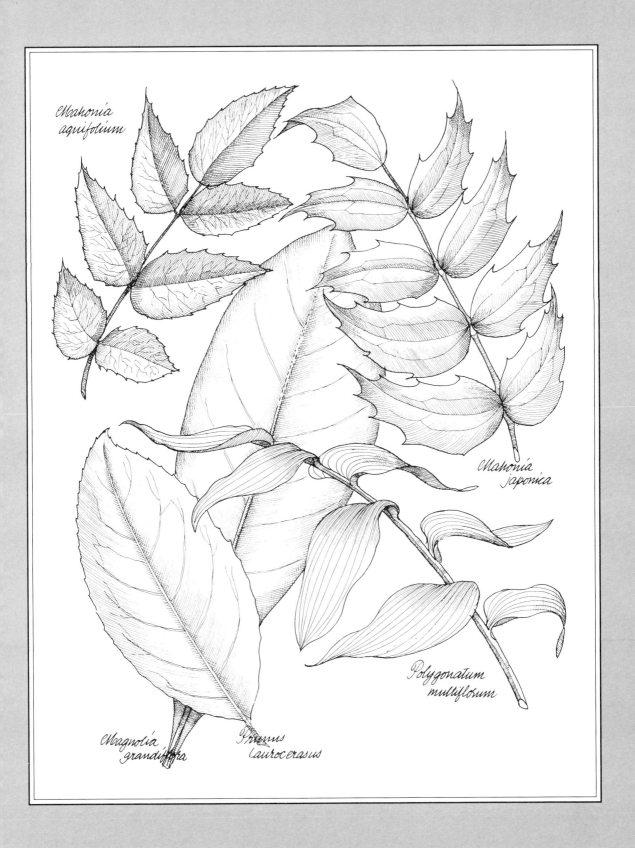

Mahonia aquifolium

Mahonia japonica

Polygonatum multiflorum

Magnolia grandiflora

Prunus Laurocerasus

QUERCUS
Q. petraea and ***Q. robur***
OAK

Both the sessile oak and the common oak are well-known deciduous trees. Their leaves are such an unusual and attractive shape that I often wonder why this foliage is not more widely used in flower arrangements. As a preserved foliage it is a particular favourite of mine.

HARVESTING AND PRESERVING Select well-shaped short branches, avoiding ones on which the growth of leaves is rather solid and clumpy. Preserve using glycerine method No. 1.

RHODODENDRON

This is a large group of shrubs, species of which are found throughout the world. As a flower arranger I look for species with good leaf formations and I have to say that I find *Rhododendron ponticum*, the well-known dark evergreen variety which has mauve flowers, the most useful for preserving, due to its leaf formation.

HARVESTING AND PRESERVING Gather in late summer, throughout autumn and early winter. You will find its dark green leathery laurel-like leaves grow in the form of a rosette around the flower buds which have already formed for the following year. Preserve complete rosettes by the glycerine method No. 1. Use the special aftercare treatment described on page 140.

ROSA
ROSE

Sprays of rose foliage are particularly useful to preserve, not only for arrangements, but also to use in winter with commercially purchased roses.

HARVESTING AND PRESERVING Carefully gather selected sprays of mature foliage from bush or rambler roses from July onwards, while the leaves remain green. Preserve using glycerine method No. 1. About one week will be sufficient to preserve the foliage while retaining its green colouring which usually only darkens slightly.

RUSCUS
R. aculeatus
BUTCHER'S BROOM

This evergreen shrub-like European plant can also be found in Britain, both in the wild and as a cultivated plant. Growing 45–90 cm ($1\frac{1}{2}$–3 ft) high, the ruscus has no true leaves but its small spiny leaf-like structures are flattened shoots called cladodes which function as leaves. The name butcher's broom originated from the custom of butchers using small bundles to sweep their cutting blocks.

R. hypoglossum

This ruscus, which is a native of Southern Europe, has larger leaves which are not spiny. My reason for including this foliage is that it is readily available from the florist, and its 'leafy' stems provide the arranger with a particularly good form.

HARVESTING AND PRESERVING The characteristic tough texture of butcher's broom enables it to be dried naturally by air method No. 1 or No. 2, while the softer texture of the *hypoglossum* responds well to glycerine method No. 2.

SEA RAGWORT

see CINERARIA

Rosa

Ruscus
aculeatus

Ruscus
hypoglossum

Quercus

Rhododendron

SKIMMIA
S. japonica

This evergreen shrub has tough glossy medium-size leaves. These are borne in a similar formation to the leaves of the rhododendron.

HARVESTING AND PRESERVING Gather short branches with complete rosettes of mature leaves at almost any time. Preserve using glycerine method No. 1. Other forms of skimmia will preserve equally well.

SPOTTED LAUREL *see AUCUBA*

SPURGE *see EUPHORBIA*

STACHYS
S. lanata
LAMB'S EARS or
LAMB'S TONGUE

A dual purpose herbaceous plant which is valuable not only for its beautiful silvery leaves but also for its stems of flower-like calcyces (see page 42).

HARVESTING AND PRESERVING As the leaves have a somewhat downy or furry texture, I prefer to preserve these using the desiccant method which retains the downy texture and also their beautiful silvery colouring. These leaves can be used either singly or by wiring several together in the form of a spray (see page 154).

STRAWBERRY TREE *see ARBUTUS*

SWEET CHESTNUT *see CASTANEA SATIVA*

TAXUS
T. baccata
YEW

This rather sombre dark evergreen tree is often associated with old churchyards where it was extensively planted in olden days. It is a foliage which I seldom see used by the flower arranger, but one which I find extremely useful when preserved. It provides large branches of feathery foliage which is particularly useful to outline a large arrangement such as a pedestal. It also provides a contrast to the many more solid forms of foliage.

HARVESTING AND PRESERVING Pick from late summer, through autumn and winter when the foliage is fully mature. Preserve using glycerine method No. 1.

TELLIMA
T. grandiflora

This plant grows well in moist conditions and is possibly more prized for its leaves than for its flowers. When fully mature the leaves of the tellima are rounded with an attractive serrated edge.

HARVESTING AND PRESERVING It is possible to preserve fully mature green leaves by glycerine method No. 2, but as I value these leaves for their colour, I use the desiccant method to preserve the deep reddish colouring of the tiny immature leaves and also many of the mature leaves which develop quite a marked salmony-red surface, particularly during the winter.

VIBURNUM
V. rhytidophyllum

This is a large wide-spreading evergreen shrub which reaches a height of 3 m (10 ft) or more. Its large eliptic leaves, up to 20 cm (8 in) long, are deeply veined giving a decorative wrinkled effect to the upper surface of the leaf. The underside is grey with a somewhat felted texture.

HARVESTING AND PRESERVING I like to preserve the foliage of this viburnum from autumn until spring during which time the branches of foliage can be gathered complete with the rusty-brown flower buds which give added interest. Preserve using glycerine method No. 1. The upper surface of the leaf will darken, but the underside will retain its colour and texture.

V. tinus

This widely grown evergreen shrub is extremely useful to preserve for filling in an arrangement, as it has rather dense foliage which is reasonably small and pliable. Use glycerine method No. 1 for preservation.

YEW *see TAXUS BACCATA*

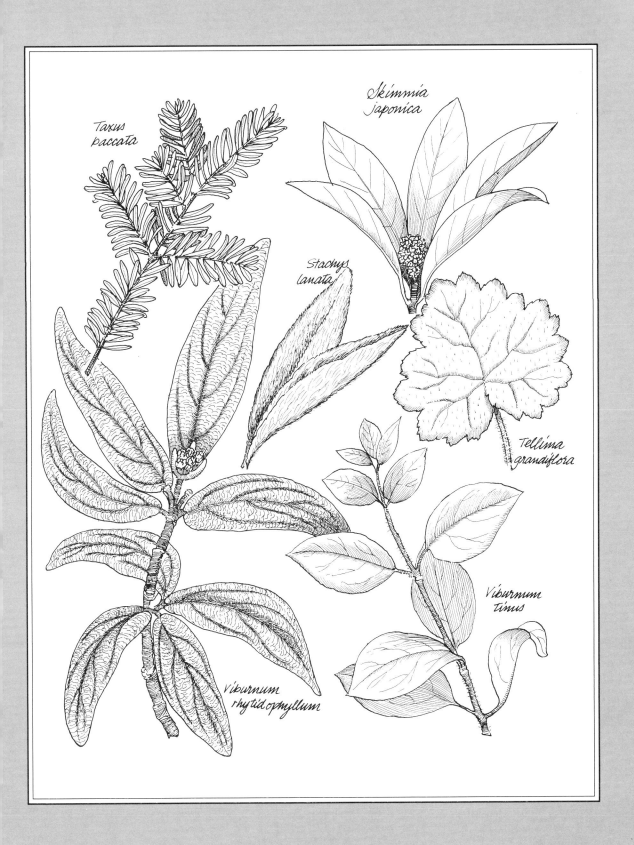

Taxus
baccata

Skimmia
japonica

Stachys
lanata

Tellima
grandiflora

Viburnum
tinus

Viburnum
rhytidophyllum

3 FLOWERING GRASSES

Including sedges and rushes

Although we may not look upon this group of plants as flowers, they do indeed form a very important part of our flora.

GRASSES Grasses are one of nature's gifts that we often take very much for granted, but, if we stop to think, we will realise just how important this family of flowering plants are to life as we know it. Take, for instance, the cereal grasses and the grasses of our meadowland and pastures. Almost everywhere we care to look we will find one or more species of grass growing on every type of soil, and often in the most barren spot.

In this book we are concerned only with the species which produce decorative flower heads, suitable for preserving.

Grasses belong to the family of flowering plants known as Gramineae, of which between 150–160 species are naturalized in the British Isles, varying in height from a few inches to several feet. Some of the smaller forms provide us with ideal material for miniature arrangements, while the taller ones can either be used mixed with other preserved materials, to give added textural interest, or arranged in a container on their own, if possible displayed against a plain background where their graceful spikelets can be shown off to their best advantage. This is how I love to see them.

At a glance it may be thought that all grasses look the same, especially when we see them in a mass, with their nodding heads waving in a gentle breeze. But if you stop and study them more closely, you will discover there are as many varieties of shape and form in our grasses as there are in our flowers. The nodding heads to which I refer are, of course, the flower heads, known as the inflorescence of the grasses, and in each case made up of many spikelets, forming either a spike-like panicle, a loose open panicle, or a raceme. At the base of each individual spikelet are two chaffy scales called glumes; these contain one or more flowers which, in many grasses, appear rather insignificant. Unlike most other flowering plants, each flower is enclosed within two more scales, called the lemma and the palea, and later, if fertile, each will produce one seed, called a grain. In many species of grass, hair-like awns will be found protruding from each spikelet, giving the grass an air of delicacy and gracefulness.

SEDGES AND RUSHES Sedges and rushes so closely resemble grasses that, to all but the botanist, it is often difficult to know when what looks like a grass is, in fact, a sedge, or rush. I think that possibly the only way to distinguish them easily from grasses is by means of the stems which are solid and often triangular, unlike the stems of most grasses which are hollow. The true sedges belong to the group of flowering plants known as Cyperaceae, while the rushes belong to the group known as Juncaceae. The flowering times are during the same season as grasses. Sedges and rushes are not generally to be found in such abundance as the grasses, and for this reason may not arouse such an interest in the flower arranger. However, within these two groups of plants are some very decorative species, a few of which I have included to show their characteristic form. The keen observer will no doubt discover many more. Although a few species grow in dry situations, it is in damp swampy places that we should concentrate our search.

THE HARVESTING OF GRASSES As a general guide harvesting should take place at flowering time, not only for the purpose of keeping the complete inflorescence intact, but also because, at this stage of growth, grasses offer a wider scope from a preservation point of view. This in turn creates a far greater interest in finished arrangements. While the majority of grasses flower in late spring and early summer, there are a few which flower later, and these include many of the annual cultivated grasses. A few of course, particularly the sedges and rushes, are more attractive when fruiting which is often not until the autumn. (See details of individual species.)

DRYING OR PRE-SERVING GRASSES

Gathered, as I have suggested, at or even before flowering time, grasses can be air dried, using method No. 1 or No. 2 depending on their form, when most of their natural colour will be retained. Alternatively, preserved by glycerine method No. 2, grasses picked at the same stage of growth will develop a beautiful silken sheen, and will, of course, be very supple to handle. the natural colouring of grasses treated in this way will be lost, but instead many will acquire a glorious golden hue which will be far richer than the natural straw colour of grasses gathered later in the season.

It is often not until later in the season, when grasses have matured and the grain ripened, that many of us think of collecting them, and so often we are disappointed when a large percentage disintegrate. With many species this is only to be expected, for, when maturity is reached, they will often break up beneath each lemma, leaving only the glumes intact. While some grasses can still be attractive at this stage, others have little left to offer in the way of beauty. However, if having left it so late, you have no alternative but to hunt for the most decorative of these forms, you have but one consolation, and that is the joy of being able to arrange them immediately wherever they are required, as nature will have completed the drying process for you. For this reason, of course, even the glycerine method will have no effect, for, as there is no moisture left in the grasses, they cannot absorb the glycerine mixture.

NOTE Grasses which are dried by the air method will need to have their foliage removed either before or after drying, as it will become brittle, shrivelled and tatty, and completely ruin their decorative qualities.

For easy reference I have divided this chapter of grasses into two parts.

Part 1: cultivated ornamental grasses

These can be either natives of other countries, or grasses which are now rarely found in the wild in Britain. As I mentioned in my introduction, the species illustrated in this section generally grow only under cultivation. It will therefore be necessary to refer to a good seedsman or plantsman's catalogue if you wish to grow these grasses which will provide you with unusual material for decorative work. Again, as with everlasting flowers, reference to these catalogues usually confronts us with a list of Latin names and, apart from a few which also have such common names as hare's tail and squirrel tail, often, in spite of very good descriptions, we are left wondering what the flower heads really look like when choosing grasses for our particular needs. I hope the illustrations combined with the following descriptions of some of the most decorative species will help you in making a selection.

BRIZA
B. maxima
LARGE QUAKING GRASS

A native of the Mediterranean region, this hardy annual is easy to grow, but prefers a light sandy soil and full sun. Larger than *B. minor* and *B. media*, which I have described in the following section, the inflorescence is borne on slender wiry branched stems, each bearing up to twelve large ovate spikelets which tremble in the slightest breeze. The characteristic formation of these is quite unique, as you will see from the illustration. Their texture could be likened to that of puffed wheat. A close-up study of the inflorescence will show an interesting variation of colouring, from green to mauve through to cream, with an over-all silken sheen.

NOTE It is of the utmost importance to gather these grasses as soon as the spikelets have completely formed, otherwise they will quite soon break up completely to release their seeds.

BROMUS
B. macrostachys

A native of southern Europe, western Asia and North Africa, this grass is cultivated as an annual. It is a delightful grass which is very conspicuous in the garden and when dried offers a contrasting form to many of the other cultivated species. The large spikelets, which have long spreading spiky awns, are carried on slender stems, but the main stem of this grass is tall and erect.

B. madritensis
COMPACT BROME

Also known as wall brome and upright brome, this grass is a native of the Mediterranean region, which can be cultivated from seed as an annual. It can also be found naturalised in a few scattered places, particularly on old walls and ruins, but it is generally considered to be rare and therefore should not be picked. This is a very decorative grass with erect panicles of spikelets which have very long fine awns, and are of a purple or green colouring. The over-all decorative effect of these grasses could be described as rather feathery.

NOTE This is another grass which must be picked early before it is mature, at which stage it will completely break up.

BROOM-CORN MILLET *see PANICUM MILIACEUM*

BULRUSH *see TYPHA*

CANARY GRASS *see PHALARIS CANARIENSIS*

COIX
C. lacryma-jobi
JOB'S TEARS

This is a plant of the tropics which, in cold climates, perhaps should be treated as half-hardy annual rather than a hardy annual. It is cultivated purely for its decorative heads of large grains, which are of course the 'tears'. When these mature in the autumn, they become very hard and of a pearl-grey or mauve colour. Protruding in racemes from their sheath-like leaves, they look like shiny beads. In fact, they are used for making rosaries and necklaces in some countries. On the whole, I consider this to be a curious and interesting grass.

COMPACT BROME *see BROMUS MADRITENSIS*

CORTADERIA
C. selloana
PAMPAS GRASS

The pampas grass originated from Argentina, its name cortaderia being derived from *cortadero* which is the Spanish name for this plant. It can often be found listed in plant catalogues as *C. argentea*. This is probably the most widely grown and universally known of all ornamental grasses, although maybe not so extensively grown now as during the Victorian era, probably due to the large amount of space that these perennial plants require. The inflorescence of the pampas grass I would describe as being in the form of a handsome plume-like head, although its true description is a loosely formed panicle. In all I believe there are thirteen varieties of this grass. Although mostly their inflorescence is silvery white in colour, I have seen some grasses that are distinctly pink. I think one such plant must be the variety 'Rosea'. Due to size the complete inflorescence is really only suitable for large arrangements, but I find it can also be extremely useful for smaller arrangements if each inflorescence is divided. This is easily done because of the branched formation of the inflorescence. In fact, one complete head can provide many small grasses simply by attaching a wire to each individual segment.

HARVESTING AND PRESERVING I feel there is only one successful way to preserve pampas grasses for use in arrangements: gather them at flowering time, but before they have completely emerged from their sheath. This is usually in late summer or early autumn. If, at this stage of growth, they are preserved by glycerine method No. 2, the beautifully silky texture of the inflorescence will be retained. Surprisingly, the colour is also retained, but, with keeping, I find these grasses become more creamy in colour, which makes them even more attractive. If you wish to have fluffy pampas grasses, gather them at the same time and preserve them using air method No. 1 or No. 2. In comparison, however, this method will produce a rather dull and dried effect.

NOTE It is very important to harvest these grasses at the stage of growth I describe above, picked later they will become very fluffy and, as they dry, they will shed bits of fluff everywhere.

FOXTAIL MILLET *see SETARIA ITALICA*

HARE'S TAIL *see LAGURUS OVATUS*

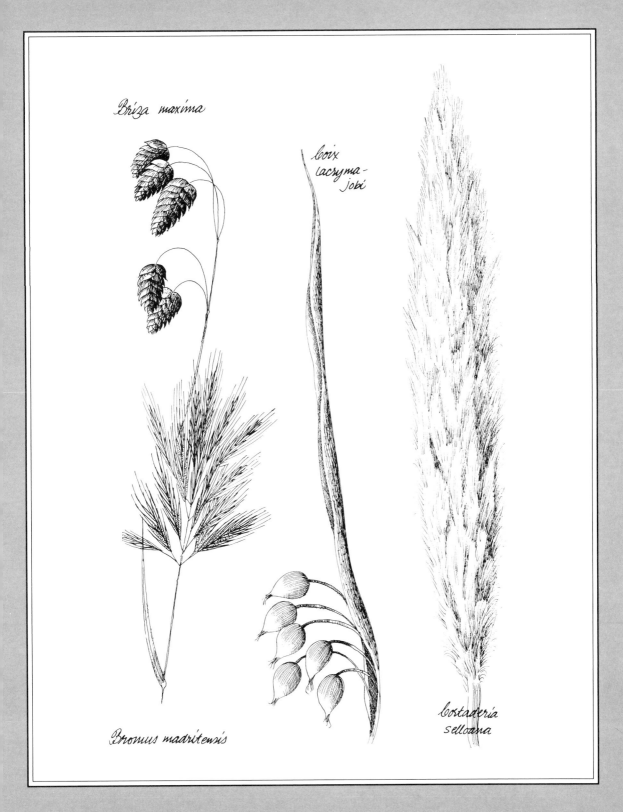

Briza maxima

Coix lacryma-jobi

Bromus madritensis

Cortaderia selloana

HORDEUM
H. jubatum
SQUIRREL-TAIL GRASS

This is also known as foxtail barley, *hordeum* being an old Latin name for barley. A native of North America, this short-lived perennial grass can be easily grown from seed. The genus Hordeum includes not only our cereal grasses *H. vulgare* and *H. distichon*, but also wall barley, *H. murinum*, which is described and illustrated in the next section on wild grasses. From a decorative point of view, the characteristics of the squirrel-tail grass differ only slightly from those of its relatives. The long awns are even longer than those of wall barley, up to 9 cm ($\frac{1}{2}$ in, and, in relation to cereal barley, the heads are less pendulous. The overall textural appearance of the inflorescence is much finer than the other varieties, each awn resembling a glistening thread of silk. Like wall barley, it is important to pick this grass early before it matures and breaks up.

JOB'S TEARS

see COIX LACRYMA-JOBI

LAGURUS
L. ovatus
HARE'S TAIL GRASS

This is a truly beautiful annual grass which is a native of the Mediterranean region. Anyone who has taken a holiday in this area will be familiar with its soft furry flowering heads, which really do resemble a hare or rabbit's tail. Hare's Tail is derived from the Greek, *lagus*, a hare, and *oura*, a tail.

L. ovatus 'Nanus'

This is a dwarf variety which never grows more than 15 cm (6 in) in height. It is a really delightful miniature version which, of course, is ideal for miniature arrangements.

ORNAMENTAL WHEAT

see TRITICUM SPELTA

PAMPAS GRASS

see CORTADERIA SELLOANA

PANICUM
P. miliaceum
syn. **P. violaceum**
BROOM-CORN MILLET

Also known by such names as common millet, hog millet and Indian millet, this tall annual grass is grown as a food crop in many parts of the world, including North America. In Britain it is grown only as a garden grass for its large graceful inflorescence, in the form of a branched pendulous panicle which is usually green, and occasionally purple. There is a definite need to gather these grasses as soon as they have completely formed, for later the spikelets will quickly shed.

PEARL GRASS

see BRIZA

PHALARIS
P. canariensis
CANARY GRASS

Phalaris is an ancient Greek name for grass and, although we are concerned with its decorative values, in warmer climates this grass is cultivated for its seeds which provide food for cage birds. This is obviously the reason why its common name is canary grass. The inflorescence is in the form of a dense ovoid spike which grows erect and is of a coarse texture, a marked contrast with the hare's tail grass. In colour the heads are green and whitish. If carefully sown in an undisturbed patch in the garden, it will continue to grow each year from self-sown seedlings (but only if you allow a few grasses to remain unpicked).

SETARIA
S. italica
FOXTAIL MILLET

This is another grass cultivated in warm countries for its seeds which provide food for cage birds. The inflorescence consists of an upright, very dense, fat, spike-like cylindrical panicle, up to 10 cm (4 in) long. However, with maturity, the stem bends with the weight of the head and the grass assumes a pendulous nature.

S. lutescens
syn. **S. glauca**
YELLOW
BRISTLE GRASS

As the name suggests, this grass bears erect spike-like panicles which have the appearance of being very brittle, although to the touch these bristles are in fact quite soft. Often wrongly identified as Timothy grass which is of the same form, but, in contrast, is a smooth-textured wild grass. The colour of the yellow bristle grass is an attractive reddish yellow.

In my original book, *Preserved Flowers*, I made the mistake of saying this grass would fall apart if left to mature which is not necessarily true, but do not leave it too long, for the sun will bleach its attractive colouring.

SQUIRREL-TAIL GRASS

see HORDEUM JUBATUM

TRITICUM
T. spelta
ORNAMENTAL WHEAT

A tall grass of up to 60 cm (2 ft) in height, *T. spelta* is a more decorative form of our cultivated bread-wheat, *T. aestivum*, which was known to have grown in the Nile Valley as long ago as 5000 BC. The formation of the spikelets in wheat is similar to barley, but each grain is larger and of a more solid appearance. The outstanding decorative quality of *T. spelta* is its exceptionally long awns.

YELLOW BRISTLE GRASS

see SETARIA LUTESCENS

Lagurus ovatus

Setaria italica

Setaria lutescens

Hordeum jubatum

Phalaris canariensis

Panicum miliaceum

Part 2: wild grasses—sedges and rushes

This part deals entirely with grasses that are to be found naturalised. These grasses can be just as decorative and graceful as the cultivated forms,but are often overlooked as they merge into the lush growth of the countryside in early summer, at a time when our eyes are turned towards the brighter colours of summer flowers.

I could not possibly hope to show illustrations of all the species; I have therefore selected many of the more decorative ones, while at the same time showing the varying forms.

AGROSTIS
A. stolonifera
CREEPING BENT

This very beautiful perennial grass is also known as fine bent and marsh bent-grass. It is common throughout Britain in wet or dry meadows, on chalk downs, in salt marshes, by roadsides and on waste ground. The inflorescence is in the form of a delicate panicle on a thin stem, 30–60 cm (1–2 ft) in height. These grasses can sometimes be found in a pale yellowish green, but quite often they are of a purplish colour. I think this difference in colour may be dependent on the various types of soil in which it grows. Unless picked early this grass will break up with maturity.

AMMOPHILA
A. arenaria
MARRAM GRASS

Known also as sea mat-grass, and in the USA as European beach-grass, the perennial marram grass is abundant on the sand dunes of the British coastline. It is a most useful plant as it acts as a stabilizer for large areas of sand dunes, and is often planted for this purpose. In contrast to the bent grasses the inflorescence of the marram grass is in the form of a close tapering panicle on a stiff erect stem, some 90–120 cm (3–4 ft) high. Although pale green when dry, these grasses quickly fade to a biscuit colour.

AVENA
A. fatua
WILD OAT

During the summer this is a common annual weed of British cornfields where it can often be seen towering above the cultivated cereal grasses, some 60–90 cm (2–3 ft) in height. It is a handsome and very decorative grass. The long stiff stems support a large spreading panicle of drooping pale green spikelets, inside of which are contrasting brown bristly tufts with long bent awns. Although very troublesome to the farmer, it is a highly decorative grass for the flower arranger, and I am sure any farmer would be more than pleased to part with as many of these grasses as you need, especially at the time when he goes 'roguing', an expression used for pulling out these wild oats before they drop their seed, which is also the ideal time to gather them.

NOTE Do not gather these without permission for fear of trampling down the cereal grasses.

BARREN BROME

see BROMUS STERILIS

BRIZA
B. minor
COMMON QUAKING GRASS

Common quaking grass is very plentiful during the month of June. Although I have only found it growing among the short grass of downlands, I read that it also grows in dry and moist meadows. Similar, but smaller, is *B. minor*, the lesser quaking grass. The name quaking grass is derived from the Greek verb 'to vibrate' which adequately describes its reaction to the slightest breeze. The delicate inflorescence of these grasses is in the form of a loose panicle on a short erect stem. The spikelets are of a purplish-brown colour and hung on hair-like branches. These dainty elegant grasses are ideal for small and miniature arrangements, but for miniatures they may need to be divided, the individual segments being attached to wires.

NOTE *B. maxima* can be found on page 76.

BROMUS
B. sterilis
BARREN BROME

Early summer is the time to look for the barren brome grass in hedgerows, on waste ground or by roadsides. This is one of Britain's most common wild grasses, but, for the flower arranger, I think it is one of the most beautiful and decorative species. The slender stem, terminating in a gracefully drooping panicle of long awned spikelets, is usually pale green, but often tinged with mauve. I find those which grow in a sunny position are usually more mauve. Although the stem of this grass grows erect, it soon flops over with the weight of its inflorescence. This often makes it difficult to find, as the true character and form of the grass is then only visible when picked. However, it usually grows in a mass and can often be identified by a haze of mauve.

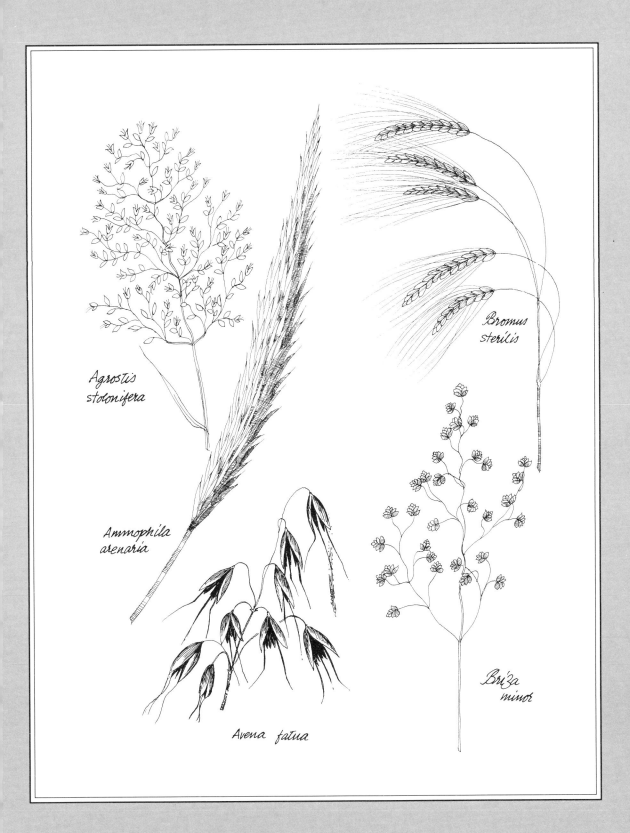

Agrostis
stolonifera

Ammophila
arenaria

Avena fatua

Bromus
sterilis

Briza
minor

CAREX
C. acutiformis
LESSER MARSH SEDGE

Found growing on the banks of rivers, canals and ditches, this tall sedge attains a height of 60–90 cm (2–3 ft). The inflorescence grows erect and is in the form of long spikelets which are cylindrical and of a brownish-green colour.

NOTE Beware of the stems, they have extremely sharp edges.

C. pendula
GREAT PENDULOUS SEDGE

The pendulous sedge is to be found in damp woods on heavy clay soil. It is one of the taller sedges, often reaching a height of $1\frac{1}{2}$ m (5 ft). The inflorescence is in the form of three or four long cylindrical spikelets which, in contrast to the lesser pond sedge, are pendulous. In colour these are a brownish-green, but at the top of each flowering stem is an erect male spikelet which is brown. It is a very graceful sedge for water scenes.

CAT'S TAIL GRASS *see PHLEUM PRATENSE*

COMMON REED *see PHRAGMITES COMMUNIS*

COMMON RYE GRASS *see DOLIUM PERENNE*

CREEPING BENT *see AGROSTIS STOLONIFERA*

ERIOPHORUM
E. vaginatum
HARE'S-TAIL
COTTON GRASS

I have only found this perennial grass on boggy moors in early summer. In this situation it is widespread in northern temperate regions. Its snow-white heads, borne on delicate stems, are beautifully soft and fluffy to the touch and, in the sunlight, they develop a glorious silken sheen. The cotton grass, of which there are other varieties, is quite unlike any other species of grass and from a distance, in mass, these grasses could be mistaken for small white flowers. On closer inspection they resemble small balls of cotton wool. You may find that you can do little more than enjoy the beauty of these grasses from a distance, as I have found that to pick them from their boggy habitat is no easy matter unless you have come prepared with adequate footwear.

FESTUCA
F. pratensis
MEADOW FESCUE

Distributed throughout Britain, this moisture-loving grass will be found growing in such places as damp hay meadows, pastures, hedgerows and riversides. Its loose nodding panicles of large spikelets are green or purplish in colour. Although similar in appearance to the barren brome, the spikelets are awnless.

GREAT SHARP SEA RUSH *see JUNCAS ACUTUS*

HARE'S-TAIL COTTON GRASS *see ERIOPHORUM VAGINATUM*

HORDEUM
H. murinum
WALL BARLEY

This annual grass is not only found in Britain but also occurs throughout much of the northern temperate zone. It grows mainly on sandy soils, in waste places and by roadsides. I have also found it in such places as the edges of car parks where it appears to grow in shallow dusty earth. Wall barley closely resembles cereal barley and, for this reason, is often referred to as wild barley. It is easily recognised by its hair-like awned inflorescence which is in the form of a cylindrical spike about (2 in) long. Although this grass flowers later than most other wild grasses, it is important to pick it before the inflorescence opens as, if picked too late, it will rapidly disintegrate.

JUNCUS
J. acutus
GREAT SHARP SEA RUSH

As its name implies, this is a rush which grows in damp sandy places near the coast. It is the largest of the native British rushes, and its flowers, which form during the summer months, are succeeded in the early autumn by crowded panicles of large glossy bright brown seed capsules. It is at this time that the sea rush is most decorative, but for anyone trying to gather them with unprotected hands, a word of warning: their stems are very sharp and they could cause a severe wound.

LESSER POND SEDGE *see CAREX ACUTIFORMIS*

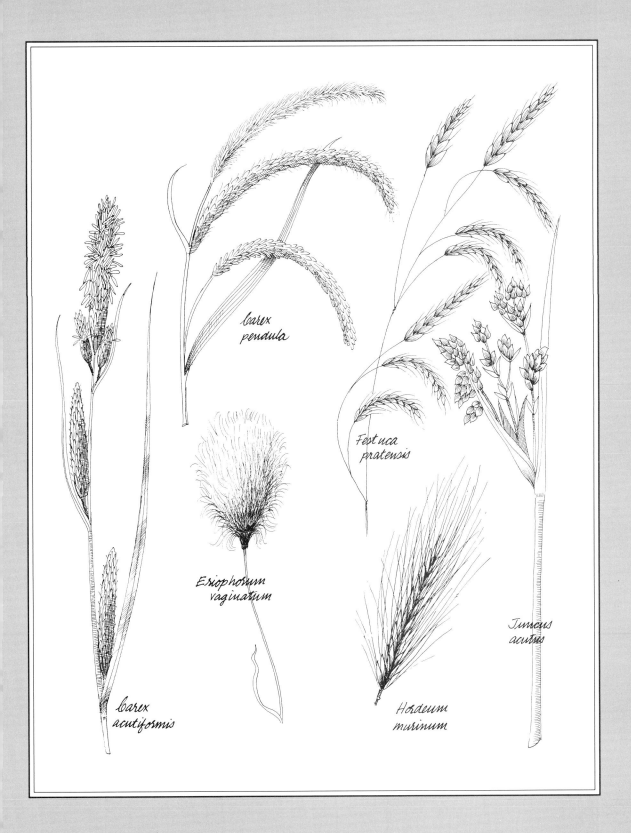

Carex
pendula

Festuca
pratensis

Eriophorum
vaginatum

Juncus
acutus

Carex
acutiformis

Hordeum
murinum

LOLIUM
L. perenne
COMMON RYE GRASS

Also known by such names as red darnel, or beardless darnel, the common rye grass is very abundant in meadow pastures and waste places. In fact, I seem mainly to gather these grasses on roadside verges. Their height varies considerably from about 15–60 cm (6–24 in), but I mainly find they reach an average height of 30 cm (12 in). The inflorescence spike is dark green with flattish spikelets arranged alternately along about a third of the stem. These are joined edge-on to the stem, giving the entire grass the appearance of having been pressed. This is a favourite grass of mine, as its form differs so much from other grasses and it can be encouraged to form graceful curves if dried by air method No. 2.

MARRAM GRASS *see AMMOPHILA ARENARIA*

MEADOW FESCUE *see FESTUCA PRATENSIS*

PENDULUS SEDGE *see CAREX PENDULA*

PHLEUM
P. pratense
COMMON CAT'S-TAIL GRASS

The common cat's-tail grass, also known as Timothy grass, is probably the one grass that everyone knows. The name Timothy arises from its connection, during the last century, with an American Mr Timothy Hanson, who took it from one State to another to investigate its potential as cattle fodder. This perennial grass has erect dense spike-like cylindrical green panicles, often tinged with pink. Its form provides contrast to many of the other, more open grasses.

PHALARIS
P. arundinacea
REED GRASS

By riversides and on marshy land this beautiful perennial grass is conspicuous in June and July when its stems rise to as much as $1\frac{1}{2}$ m (5 ft) high, with erect pale green panicles tinged with purple. Although similar to the true reed described below, I feel this grass retains a more open structure and its spikelets have a more distinct form, rather than appearing as tufts.

PHRAGMITES
P. communis
COMMON REED

Areas of common reed are a familiar sight by lakes and rivers. I have also found them growing in boggy ditches. In late summer the large erect purplish-brown plumes can be seen swaying in the breeze. It is important to gather it at this early stage of growth if the beauty of its colouring is to be retained. A little later and the numerous long narrow tufty spikelets appear greyish, owing to the growth of long silky hairs. Although at this stage of growth it will not readily disintegrate, it is more solid, less graceful and certainly less colourful.

Readers of my book, *Making Animal and Bird Collages,* with grasses, leaves, seedheads and cones, will know how I have found the common reed invaluable to represent the fur of cats, mice, rabbits etc. For larger flower arrangements it is also valuable, particularly for water scenes.

QUAKING GRASS *see BRIZA MEDIA*

REEDMACE *see TYPHA*

REED GRASS *see PHALARIS ARUNDINACEA*

RYE GRASS *see LOLIUM PERENNE*

TIMOTHY GRASS *see PHLEUM PRATENSE*

TYPHA
REEDMACE

I feel the reedmace belongs to this section from a flower arranger's point of view, although it is neither a sedge nor a rush, but in fact belongs to the family of plants known as Typhacae. I only know of the following two species, but I have discovered there are, in fact, about nine distributed throughout the world.

T. angustifolia
LESSER REEDMACE

As its name suggests, this is the smaller of the two species, but it is not common in Britain. It is imported, however, and is often available in its natural state from florists' shops.

T. latifolia
GREAT REEDMACE

There is often some confusion over the identity of this plant. Most of us refer to it as the bulrush, but in fact the true common bulrush is *Scirpus lacustris* and belongs to the family of plants known as Cyperaceae. Its panicle of oval-shaped spikelets bears no resemblance to the other reedmaces.

I am sure a further description of the reedmace is unnecessary, but in view of the many questions I have received on keeping them, I think a few details on harvesting would be helpful. Gather when the male inflorescence is coming into flower, this being the slender terminal spike above the dense cylindrical head of the female inflorescence. This is important, as, if gathered later, the dark brown fruiting mass will eventually break up to release its seeds.

WALL BARLEY *see HORDEUM MURINUM*

WILD OAT *see AVENA FATUA*

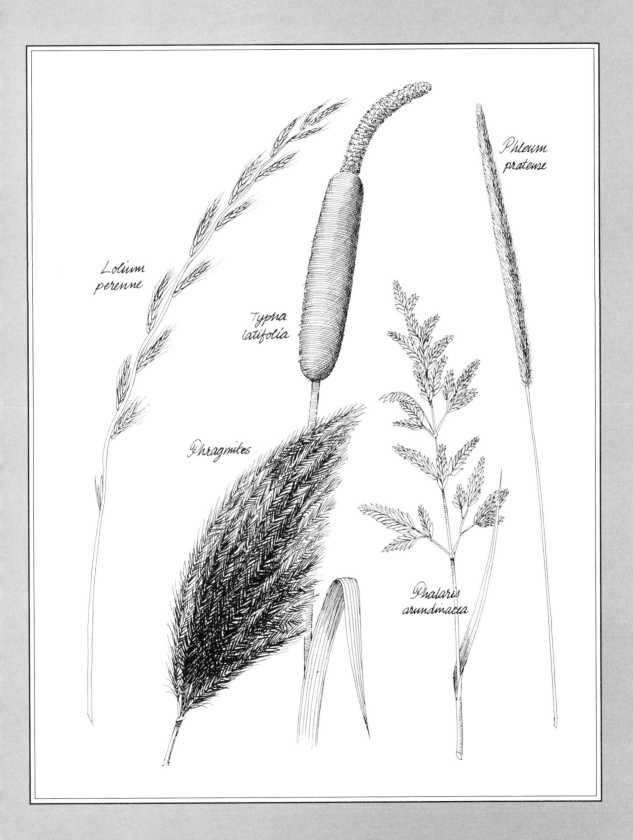

Lolium
perenne

Typha
latifolia

Phragmites

Phleum
pratense

Phalaris
arundinacea

Allium species

4 FRUITS

Seedheads, cones, hard fruits and succulent berries

The fruits of flowering plants and trees develop in many remarkable ways and this section of botany makes a fascinating study for those sufficiently interested. In this book, however, we are dealing with fruits suitable for preservation, purely from an artistic angle, for the colour, textural or architectural value they contribute to preserved work. I have divided this chapter into three sections in an attempt to provide a relatively simple reference.

Seedheads

The gathering of seedheads by the flower arranger is often limited to a few tried and trusted old favourites such as poppy and honesty seedpods. The keen observer, however, will discover many more.

It would be impossible to list and illustrate all the seedheads that are suitable for preserved work. It is, however, important to make full use of the different shapes, forms and textures of the various types of seedheads, and, to help create an awareness of these, I have written a brief description of each group and illustrated a carefully chosen selection of seedheads within each group.

ROUND HEADS These include both large and small seedheads of a rather solid appearance, also globular seedheads which consist of a ball-shaped cluster of seeds borne on a slender stalk and all radiating from the same point on the main stem. Umbelliferous seedheads differ from these, due to the seed clusters forming a rounded, but somewhat flattish, head.

SPIKY HEADS This group should include seedheads which are of a rather pointed structure, with seedpods borne singly, on either a single or branched stem. It also includes round and pointed seed capsules, of which there are many, situated at intervals close to either a single or branched stem. Many of these individual seed capsules are extremely interesting in themselves as each one is made up of several individual valves each containing many seeds. When ripe these valves become dry and split open to release their seeds, at which time they provide us with yet another form.

DENSE PANICLES AND PLUMES I feel this group is really self-explanatory, for it includes seedheads which are branched and generally crowded with seeds.

BEARDED HEADS These differ enormously from other forms of seedheads, but are only characteristic of a very few plants. The seeds form in clusters, on either single or branched heads, each seed having a bearded style which is long and slightly twisted, giving the complete head a curious twisted whirl effect.

HARVESTING Many seedheads are useful purely for their interesting forms and architectural quality. These can be harvested after they have released their seeds, when nature has already dried many of them to an almost wood-like texture. In fact, some seedcases have a more attractive shape and form after they have opened. Other seedheads, often those of a more delicate structure, can be gathered just as they approach maturity, but before the seeds ripen. At this stage we are able to capture their subtle colourings and beautiful markings. Seedheads of all types are grouped under two headings—wild and cultivated.

WILD SEEDHEADS Fortunately many of the most interesting wild seedheads are produced by the most common of our wild plants, of which many are often considered to be 'just weeds', and for this reason they are not classified as protected species. Common sense prevails here. If large quantities of the plant are to be found, this usually means it is safe to gather, but an isolated plant could well mean that it is a rare species. If in doubt, a wild-plant reference book should be consulted. It is however important to pick even the most common seedheads with care, shaking out the seeds if ripe and gathering unripe seedheads in limited quantities, leaving sufficient for the reproductive cycle to continue. Wild seedheads are not only available to country dwellers, but also to those who live in the more developed areas of our towns and cities where many seedheads are close at hand. Waste ground or ground cleared for building, even edges of car parks, are all good collecting grounds.

CULTIVATED SEEDHEADS These not only develop on the shrubs and plants of our flower gardens, but the kitchen garden too can yield many quite remarkable seedheads. It should also be remembered that a cultivated plant in our own country is in fact a native wild plant in another part of the world.

ALLIARIA
A. peliolata
GARLIC MUSTARD

This is a common spring-flowering biennial plant of hedgerows and very much a weed in many shady places including deciduous woodlands. It is also known as Jack-by-the-hedge. Being a member of the same group of plants as the wallflower which, botanically, is known as Cruciferae, it also has the same flowering habit. Starting with a small cluster of flowers, the plant continues to produce flowers along an extended stem and is often still flowering as seedpods begin to form on the lower part of the stem. During the summer, elongated seedpods develop along the entire stem.

HARVESTING AND PRESERVING Picked before they open, the seedpods are an interesting shade of mauve. Picked just as they are opening to release their little black seeds, a delicate translucent silvery central membrane will be revealed. At both stages of growth they dry easily by air method No. 1 or No. 2.

ALLIUM

This is a large group of bulbous plants which can be easily identified by their characteristic onion smell. Some of these are grown as vegetables, others as herbaceous plants. The most spectacular of all the alliums is probably *Allium giganteum*, with each individual head measuring as much as 30 cm (12 in) across. Although ideal with which to create a spectacular effect, some of the slightly smaller species are more useful, particularly *Allium aflatunense*. Although these seedheads are attractive at their green stage, they are particularly interesting when the individual capsules mature and dry. At this stage they open to reveal tiny black seeds, *Allium siculum*, with its rocket-shaped seedheads, always reminds me of fairy castles. It certainly provides unusual-shaped seedheads for small arrangements. The garden leek is also a member of the allium family that can be relied upon to produce large, rather solid-looking, globular heads if a few are allowed to remain in the garden beyond the kitchen vegetable stage.

HARVESTING AND PRESERVING Gather at any time after the seedheads have formed and dry using air method No. 2 or No. 3. When dry they lose their onion smell.

NOTE The common chive from the vegetable garden is also very decorative but at its flowering stage as is *Allium sphaerocephalium* (see page 14).

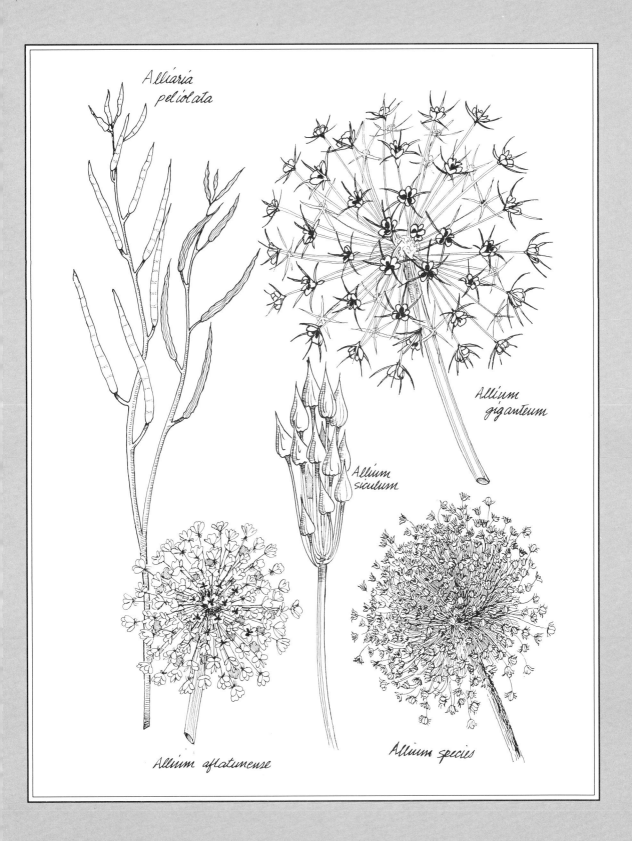

Alliaria
peliolata

Allium
giganteum

Allium
siculum

Allium aflatunense

Allium species

ANEMONE
A. pulsatilla
PASQUE FLOWER

This native British plant is grown as an early-flowering garden plant. Its beautiful mauve flowers in April and May are followed by bearded globular seedheads, each with a stiff straight stem.

HARVESTING AND PRESERVING To preserve these successfully, they must be gathered and treated by glycerine method No. 2 as soon as they have formed. Picked later they will break up.

ANGELICA
A. sylvestris
WILD ANGELICA

This is a common perennial plant found growing in wet meadows, marshes, fens, ditches and around the edges of lakes. Tall and robust it grows more than (6 ft) in height and flowers from July to September.

HARVESTING AND PRESERVING Gather these seedheads when they are fully mature. The radiating stems which form the umbrella shape will then be firm and rigid. At this stage of growth they will be an attractive mauveish-green shade. Also collect some which are turning a delightful honey colour, but do make sure the seeds are still firmly attached. Remember it is at this stage of growth that the plant prepares to release its seeds. These seedheads will dry naturally by air method No. 1, but I prefer to use glycerine method No. 2 which ensures that the seeds remain supple, and that the complete head remains intact.

NOTE The cultivated form of angelica, *A. officinalis*, also produces decorative heads which can be preserved in the same way.

AQUILEGIA
A. vulgaris
COLUMBINE

I always think of this hardy perennial as an old cottage-garden flower. Maybe this is because, as a child, I used to know it as granny's bonnet, which is certainly a very apt description of its flowers. I still grow this original form with dark violet, blue, pink or white flowers, but today the more colourful long-spurred hybrids are more generally grown. After flowering, both forms produce interesting and dainty seedheads on branched stems. Each seedhead consists of five valves, and, when mature, the opened valves resemble an attractive five-petal flower-like form.

HARVESTING AND PRESERVING Gather as the seed capsules begin to open and dry by air method No. 1 or No. 2.

ARTEMISIA

There are several herbaceous forms of this plant which produce extremely useful and decorative flower or seed panicles which, in some varieties, such as 'Lambrook Silver' are often of a rather pendulous nature, due to their rather floppy habit of growth.

A. absinthium
WORMWOOD

The structure and growth of this artemisia is not unlike *A. vulgaris,* but its over-all colouring is more silvery, with a whiteish underside to its leaves.

A. vulgaris

This is a common plant of roadsides and waste ground where it flowers from July to September. Although found growing on most types of soil, it is perhaps most frequently found on calcareous soils. A tall perennial, reaching a height of 90 cm (3 ft) or more, it is of a more erect habit of growth than most of the cultivated forms of artemisia and, unlike the cultivated forms, the over-all effect is that of a reddish-green.

HARVESTING AND PRESERVING As all the artemisias have rather insignificant flowers, the over-all effect differs little from flower to seed stage, making it possible to preserve either flower or seedhead. Use air method No. 1 or No. 2 and, when dry, remove the foliage which will be brittle and rub off easily. For more supple spikes, use glycerine method No. 2 which will also preserve the small leaves successfully.

ARTICHOKE

see GLOBE ARTICHOKE

ARUNCUS
GOAT'S BEARD

For many years known as *Spiraea aruncus,* the tall creamy white plumes of this summer-flowering perennial develop into extremely useful and decorative seed plumes.

HARVESTING AND PRESERVING I find glycerine method No. 2 the most satisfactory to use as it retains the characteristic form of the seedheads which will also remain beautifully supple.

Anemone
pulsatilla

Aruncus

Angelica
sylvestris

Artemisia
vulgaris

Artemisia
absinthium

ASTILBE
FALSE GOAT'S BEARD

There are many varieties of this summer-flowering moisture-loving plant. Although I value the astilbes for their feathery flower heads, they all produce excellent seed plumes which are similar in form to those of the aruncus.

HARVESTING AND PRESERVING While still green, these seed plumes can be preserved by glycerine method No. 2. Later, when brown, they must be air-dried by method No. 1 or No. 2. Once they have reached this stage, it is possible to gather them well into the winter months without disintegration.

CAPE GOOSEBERRY

see PHYSALIS (page 36)

CARDOON

see CYNARA CARDUNCULUS

CHAEMERION
C. augustifolium
ROSEBAY WILLOW HERB

Also known as fireweed, this tall perennial wild plant flowers from June to September when its spikes of magenta flowers are a blaze of colour. Not only is this plant common in woodland clearings, but large colonies spring up on heathland after fire has destroyed vegetation, hence its common name of fireweed. In towns and cities, too, its brilliance can often transform waste ground. After the flowers have faded, long slender seed capsules form, and, if we watch, when ripe these will split open to release the fluffy seeds. In doing so each half curls back on itself, and, as a result, the once spiky head becomes a curly plume which is rather unusual and yet probably accessible to almost everyone.

HARVESTING AND PRESERVING Gather at any time after the seed capsules have opened. It may be necessary to pull out the fluffy seeds if the wind has not taken care of this for you. Dry using air method No. 2. Alternatively, arrange them straightaway, using them at the back of an arrangement to show their delicate form. These also look good if sprayed white and arranged on their own.

CHINESE LANTERN

see PHYSALIS (page 36)

CLEMATIS

Of the many and varied forms of the climbing clematis, some produce exceptionally beautiful bearded seedheads which are very much like those of *Anemone pulsatilla. C. tangutica* is one of the most outstanding, with yellow bell-shaped flowers which later develop into large bearded seedheads.

C. vitalba
OLD MAN'S BEARD
or TRAVELLER'S JOY

A delightful wild form of clematis which grows prolifically on calcareous soil, where it climbs and cascades over trees and shrubs, sometimes completely enveloping them. The trailing stems carry clusters of bearded seedheads (hence its name) in the autumn.

HARVESTING AND PRESERVING Gather cultivated seedheads at the same stage and preserve in the same way as for *Anemone pulsatilla*. Trailing stems or short individual stems of the wild clematis can also be preserved in this way. These will develop a glorious sheen if gathered well before they show any sign of turning fluffy.

COLUMBINE

see AQUILEGIA

CONEFLOWER

see RUDBECKIA

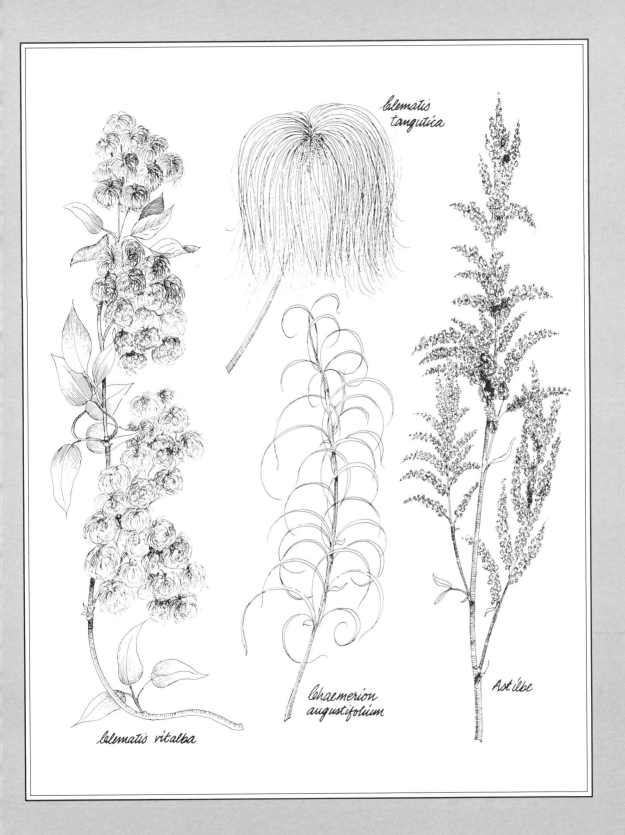

Clematis
tangutica

Chaemerion
augustifolium

Astilbe

Clematis vitalba

CROCOSMIA
MONTBRETIA

The late-summer flowering montbretias with their heads of orange flowers should never be cut down when the flowers are over, as the graceful arching spiky sprays of both the small- and large-flowered varieties produce numerous small tan-coloured knobbly seed pods.

HARVESTING AND PRESERVING Apart from looking attractive in the garden in the autumn, enhanced by the autumn sunshine, if picked when fully formed, but while still colourful, they dry very easily by air method No. 1 or No. 2 and provide an unusual and colourful form for arrangements.

CYNARA
C. cardunculas
CARDOON

This half-hardy herbaceous perennial from southern Europe and North Africa belongs to the same group of plants as the globe artichoke. Its branched leaf stalks were at one time used as a vegetable, but today it is used not so much by the cook as the flower arranger who particularly values it for its decorative silver foliage. The cardoon also produces large spiny seedheads which dry well and are of great architectural value in an arrangement.

HARVESTING AND PRESERVING There are three possible methods to follow.

1. Due to the particularly firm texture of their spiny bracts, the unopened buds of the cardoon can be gathered and preserved by air method No. 1.

2. Gather them just as the flower is fading but while the head is still green. After air drying by method No. 1 for several weeks, the withered flower petals can be pulled out to reveal a beautiful golden central seed boss surrounded by a disc of inner bracts which have a beautiful silvery sheen.

3. Leave the plant until the seedhead is ripe, by which time the petals will have withered and the head will have become hard and dry, but will have lost its green colouring. Again air dry for several weeks, after which time, in addition to removing the withered petals, take off the spiny bracts leaving only a ring of them round the stem to support the head. You will now be left with a rather attractive golden hairy boss that will provide a unique feature for an arrangement.

NOTE To ensure that the head remains intact, run a little clear adhesive around the boss.

C. scolymus
GLOBE ARTICHOKE

The globe artichoke is often confused with the cardoon. Admittedly it belongs to the same family and its appearance is similar, and it is also a native of southern Europe and North America. However, the illustration shows clearly that the globe artichoke has more rounded bracts than the cardoon. These are characteristically petal-shaped and non-spiny which gives the unopened heads a distinctive flower-like form.

HARVESTING AND PRESERVING Its decorative flower heads develop in the same way as the cardoon and should be preserved in the same way and at the same stages of growth.

NOTE Unlike the cardoon, the unopened heads of the globe artichoke are edible.

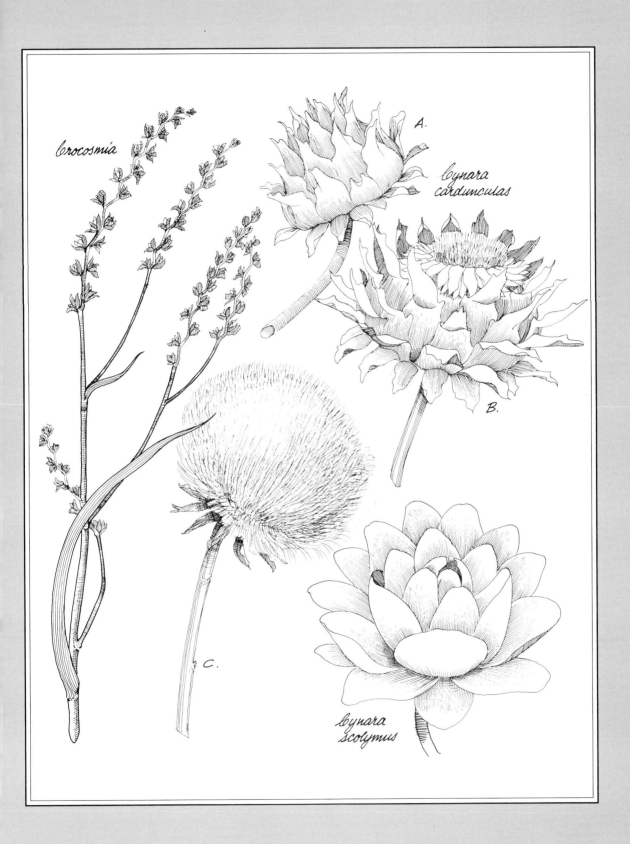

Crocosmia

A.

Cynara
cardunculas

B.

C.

Cynara
scolymus

DELPHINIUM Not only valuable for its flowers (see page 24), after flowering the delphinium produces attractive spikes of three-valved seedcases. After opening to release their seeds, these become almost flower-like.

HARVESTING AND PRESERVING These graceful spikes of seedcases can be gathered any time after they have opened: even after they have been bleached by the autumn winds and rain they still remain attractive. Dry by air method No. 1 or No. 2. Gathered in late autumn on a dry day, delphinium seedcases will usually have dried naturally and be ready for immediate use.

DIPSACUS
D. fullonum
TEASEL The teasel is a common wild plant, also known as fuller's teasel. The flowering heads are cylindrical in shape and grow erect on tall stiff stems. They are very evenly covered with spines which are more correctly termed bracts. When in flower these spines are reasonably soft, but, with maturity, and after flowering, they become stiff and needle-like. Once used by manufacturers of woollen cloth to raise a 'nap' on their fabrics, to the flower arranger they are valued purely for their decorative form.

HARVESTING AND PRESERVING As a general rule teasels should be gathered after the flowers have faded, when the heads are mature and firm, having developed their characteristic needle-like texture. Use air method No. 1 or No. 2. I also like to pick some at the flowering stage and preserve them using air method No. 1. Although the flowers will eventually fade, they retain their green colouring for a long time. Leave them hanging long enough to ensure the flower stem, just below the head, is dry and rigid to avoid it flopping.

DOCK *see RUMEX*

EVENING PRIMROSE *see OENOTHERA*

FALSE GOAT'S BEARD *see ARUNCUS*

FIELD PENNY CRESS *see THLASPI ARVENSE*

FILIPENDULA
F. ulmaria
MEADOW SWEET Meadowsweet is usually found in meadows, near water or on moist wayside verges. It grows from 60–90 cm (2–3 ft) high and produces panicles of beautiful creamy white flowers which later develop into panicles of fascinating little seeds, each resembling a tiny coil.

HARVESTING AND PRESERVING I have only had success with these by gathering them as soon as the seeds form, and while they are still green. Preserve them using glycerine method No. 2. This will ensure that they remain intact.

NOTE If picked after they have turned brown and dried on the plant, they will most certainly disintegrate.

GARLIC MUSTARD *see ALLIARIA PETIOLATA*

GLOBE ARTICHOKE *see CYNARA SCOLYMUS*

GOAT'S BEARD *see ARUNCULUS*

GRAPE HYACINTH *see MUSCARI*

GREAT MULLEN *see VERBASCUM*

HONESTY *see LUNARIA*

HOP *see HUMULUS*

HUMULUS
HOP A perennial rambling climber, the hop is a native of Europe (including Great Britain) Asia and North America. Cultivated varieties of hop have been used in the brewing of beer since the sixteenth century. From July to September, the female fruiting heads of the hop are very decorative as they hang like tiny lanterns on the long twining branched stems. Each lantern-like shape consists of small green overlapping bracts which completely conceal the fruits.

HARVESTING AND PRESERVING Gather when fully formed and mature. I would advise stem lengths of not more than 30 cm (12 in). Remove the leaves and preserve using glycerine method No. 2 which produces an attractive russet colouring. Air method No. 1 can also be used, which will retain the green colouring for some time, although they will eventually turn cream.

NOTE The annual hop can also be preserved in the same way.

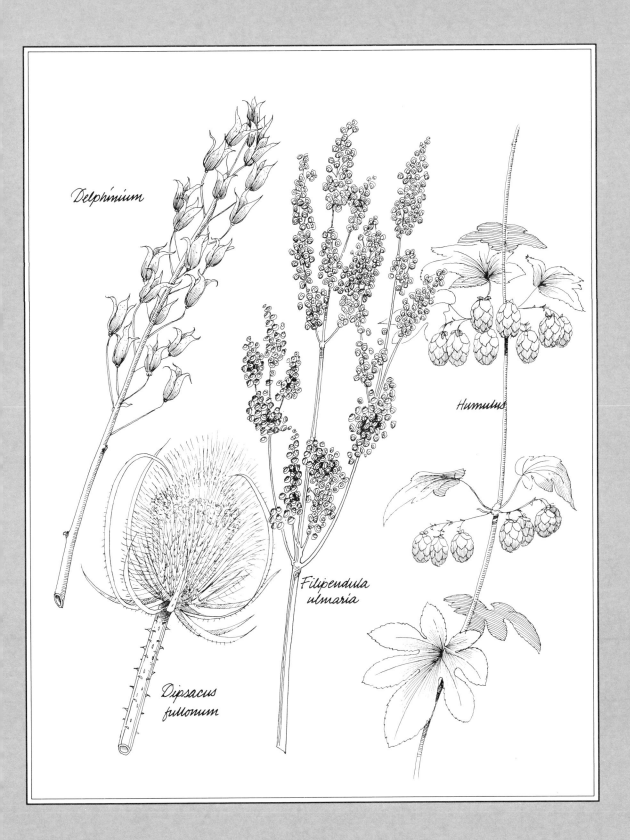

Delphinium

Filipendula
ulmaria

Dipsacus
fullonum

Humulus

HYPERICUM
H. perforatum
ST JOHN'S WORT

There are many wild varieties of St John's wort, with their bright golden star-like flowers borne on stiff erect branched stems. *H. perforatum,* being the largest form, produces extremely attractive seedheads which I think are well worth looking for.

HARVESTING AND PRESERVING These dry naturally on the plant to a golden brown, making it easy to pick and arrange them without any special treatment.

IRIS

Unfortunately, beautiful as they are, the flowers of both the wild and cultivated irises must be enjoyed either growing or as a cut flower. The fleshy texture of their petals makes them unsuitable for preserving. However, many irises more than make up for this by later rewarding us with interesting seedpods or empty seed capsules.

I. foetidissima
STINKING IRIS

This is a wild iris, found growing mainly on calcareous soils. In May it produces mauve flowers which are followed by large seed pods consisting of three valves. When ripe, these valves open, each revealing two rows of large orange-red seeds.

HARVESTING AND PRESERVING Gather just as they are opening and use air method No. 2. These highly decorative seedheads may need a coat of clear matt varnish to ensure the seeds remain securely within the seedpods. Even when given this protective coat, the seeds will eventually shrivel. At this stage I remove the seeds and use the empty dried seedcases which have a creamy felt-like lining and are extremely attractive.

I. kaempferi

This is the Japanese iris which is often grown as a bog plant at the edge of a pond. It is one of the many tuberous and fibrous-rooted species of iris which produce decorative seed capsules which mature to an almost woody structure. Being unfamiliar with many of these irises, I am not able accurately to identify the iris capsule illustrated as that of *kampferi,* but I gathered a collection of these pods from the edge of a friend's pond and they do seem to fit the description of *kaempferi.* As far as I am aware all the species within this group of irises produce similar-shaped three-valved seed capsules which are all decorative, although some are less rounded and more slender.

HARVESTING AND PRESERVING These seed capsules usually dry naturally on the plant, after which they are ready for use.

LAPSANA
L. communis
NIPPLEWORT

Nipplewort is common everywhere and, when in flower, has tiny yellow dandelion-like flowers borne on branched stems. The seedheads which form are particularly dainty and provide ideal outline material for a small arrangement.

HARVESTING AND PRESERVING It is possible to gather the stems of empty seedcases as late as November or December, by which time they will have dried naturally on the plant.

LOTUS LILY *see NELUMBO*

LOVE-IN-A-MIST *see NIGELLA*

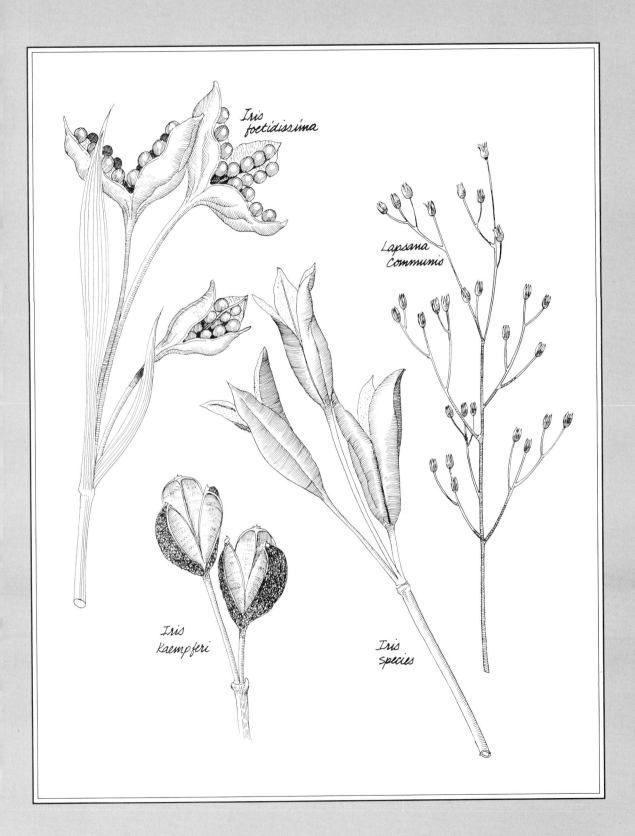

Iris
foetidissima

Lapsana
Communis

Iris
Kaempferi

Iris
species

LUNARIA
HONESTY (Money Plant)

A native of Sweden, *L. annua* syn. *L. biennis* is a well-known hardy biennial plant belonging to the wallflower family. There is also a perennial form, *L. rediviva,* which is a native of Europe. In late spring and early summer the purplish lilac wallflower-like flowers are followed by large flat pods which are of a greenish-mauve colouring. Later, as these pods dry on the plant, they lose this attractive subtle colouring.

HARVESTING AND PRESERVING I like to gather some seedheads during early summer and dry them by air method No. 1. This will retain the lovely colouring of the pods. If, however, the outer discs of the pods are peeled off and the seeds removed, an inner disc, which is a most delicate translucent green, will be revealed. If picked at the later stage and dried in the same way, the removal of the papery dry outer disc and seeds will reveal the better-known silvery translucent inner disc.

MAGNOLIA

The magnolias, thought to be among the earliest of primitive flowering plants, are truly magnificent trees, but, due to their large succulent petals, I have had little success in preserving these beautiful flowers. However, there are many forms and I am still hoping. I have included the magnolia in this section as some forms produce large, very striking, cone-like seedheads, an example of which is illustrated. To me its woody structure has a beautifully sculptured quality, reminiscent of a carved masterpiece.

HARVESTING AND PRESERVING When the seeds have been released, the seedheads will become hard and dry and need little attention other than wiring for use in arrangements or swags.

MEADOWSWEET   *see FILIPENDULA*

MONTBRETIA   *see CROCOSMIA*

MUGWORT   *see ARTEMISIA*

MULLEIN   *see VERBASCUM*

MUSCARI
M. armeniacum
GRAPE HYACINTH

Among the earliest of spring-flowering bulbs, the grape hyacinth is certainly one of the best known.

HARVESTING AND PRESERVING If left on the plant until early summer, the grape hyacinth's delicate seedpods will have opened to release their tiny black seeds and will have dried naturally to a pale parchment colour, ready for use. The structure of each individual seedcase is very reminiscent of a tiny flower.

NELUMBO
N. pentapetala syn. **N. lutea**
LOTUS LILY

This is a North American water plant, the large yellow flowers of which are similar to those of the water lily, but, unlike the water lily, after flowering it produces a large inverted conical seedhead up to 10 cm (4 in) across which contains edible nut-like fruits recessed in deep holes. These are evenly distributed over the seedhead's broad surface which is no doubt the reason for it to be known as pondnuts. It is also known by such names as wankapin and water chinquapin.

It is the mature empty seedcases that are of interest to the flower arranger, but, in Britain, these hard woody structures, which I feel are curious rather than beautiful, can only be purchased from a florist, or any other source that sells imported dried plant materials.

NOTE At the time of writing they appear to be not quite as popular as in previous years.

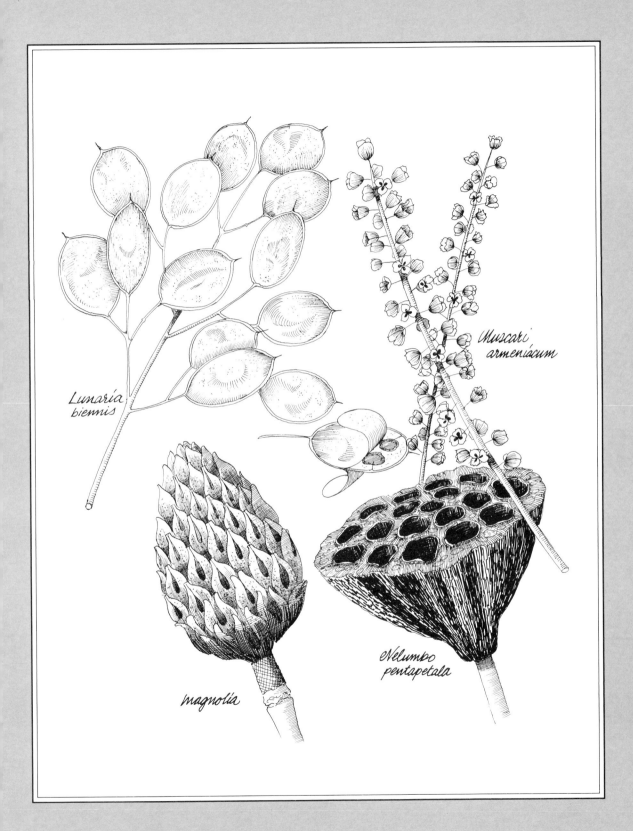

Lunaria
biennis

Muscari
armeniacum

magnolia

Nelumbo
pentapetala

NIGELLA
N. damascena
LOVE-IN-A-MIST

The attractive cornflower-blue semi-double flowers of the well-known hardy annual flowers in my garden each summer without fail, from self-sown seedlings. It must be some twenty years or more since I actually sowed seeds of this plant. It produces much finer blooms if treated in this way, and also ensures that the inflated seedpods are allowed to develop, which, when fully mature have a distinctive purple and green colouring to them.

HARVESTING AND PRESERVING If gathered as soon as they are mature (but after you have scattered the seeds), the beautiful mauve and green colouring of the pods can be retained by air method No. 1 or No. 2. Remove the foliage which will become brittle after drying. If picked at the same stage and preserved by glycerine method No. 2, the natural colouring of the pods will be lost, as they develop a greeny cream shade, but, with its rufflet of finely cut fennel-like foliage, the complete seedhead will remain soft and pliable and is most attractive.

NIPPLEWORT

see LAPSANA

OENOTHERA
O. cinaeus
EVENING PRIMROSE

This is the common yellow evening primrose which is a native of North America, although, as a garden plant, it is listed as a perennial. I find it self-seeds and grows as a biennial.

HARVESTING AND PRESERVING Evening primrose seedheads can be gathered at two stages of growth. When the entire spike of seedcases is fully formed but still tightly closed. At this stage the seed capsules will retain their attractive green and brown striped markings. Or later, when the mature capsules turn brown and open to release their seeds; at this stage of growth the seed spike relies on its decorative form rather than its colour, as the opened capsule takes on the appearance of a four-petalled flower. These are particularly attractive when given a light spray of white paint, and are extremely useful to provide height to a Christmas arrangement. Seedheads gathered at both stages of growth are dried by air method No. 1 or No. 2.

OLD MAN'S BEARD

see CLEMATIS VITALBA

PAEONIA
PEONY

Apart from the species of peonies which produce excellent flowers for preserving, there are others which develop particularly striking seedpods. The hardy perennial _P. mlokosewitschii,_ with its large single lemon-yellow flowers, I find is not really suitable for preserving. But, in the early autumn, the dull greenish-brown velvety seedpods of this species are particularly striking, as their woody structure opens to reveal a bright cerise inner lining which has a unique crumpled texture. Around the edge of each individual section, black and cerise seeds are attached.

HARVESTING AND PRESERVING Gather as the seedpods begin to split open and dry by air method No. 2. I find these seed pods, complete with seeds, can be used for quite a long time and are extremely decorative. However, eventually the seeds will fall out, leaving a knobby edging, by which time the colour of the inner surface of this seedpod will have become more subdued. It is at this stage I find these seedpods most attractive, as they have the appearance of being lined with crushed velvet.

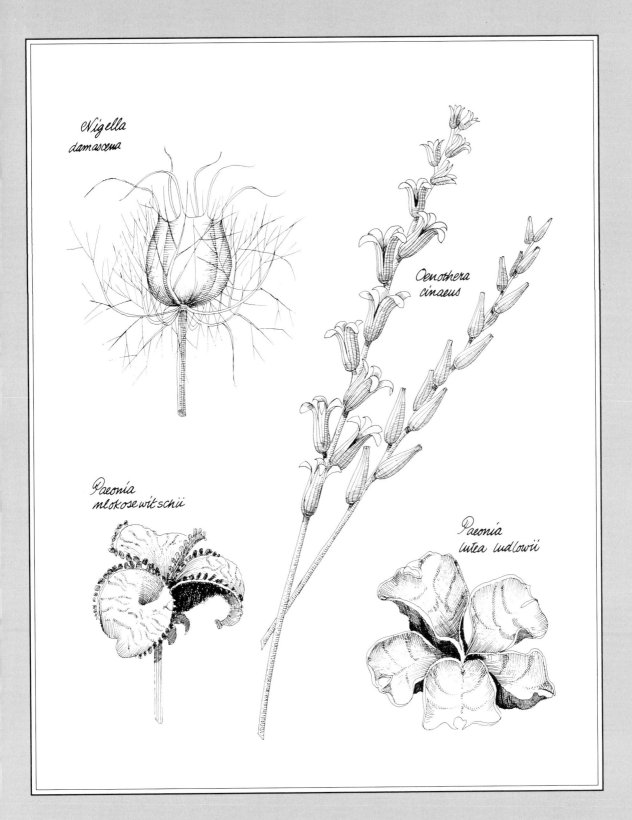

Nigella
damascena

Oenothera
cinaeus

Paeonia
mlokosewitschii

Paeonia
lutea ludlowii

PAPAVER
POPPY

This is a group of plants which includes both the cultivated and wild poppies. Cultivated varieties, which produce excellent pods for drying and preserving, include the oriental poppy which is a perennial, flowering in late spring to early summer. There are also annual poppies to grow from seed, the double variety 'Pink Chiffon', which has beautiful double peony-like flowers, comes up in my garden year after year from self-sown seedlings. Some seem to revert to single blooms, but all produce good seedpods of varying sizes. The wild poppies are of course single and have smaller seedpods which are rather more elongated than their cultivated relatives, and ideal for miniature arrangements.

HARVESTING AND PRESERVING It is important to allow poppy seedheads to become hard and mature before gathering. This will be at the time the tiny valves around the top are due to open and release the seeds. Shake out all the seeds of the annual and wild varieties to enable next year's seedlings to germinate. Dry some, using air method No. 1, to retain their grey-green colouring, and also preserve some, using glycerine method No. 2. These will turn a mauveish-grey shade which I find very pleasing.

PASQUE FLOWER *see ANEMONE PULSATILLA*

PEONY *see PAEONY*

PHYSALIS FRANCHETTI (see page 36)

PLANTAGO
P. major
GREATER PLANTAIN

A perennial wild plant, characteristic of paths and tracks. It is also common in waste places and by roadsides. Its slender flowering spikes differ little in form from its seed spikes.

HARVESTING AND PRESERVING Gather when the frothy flower mass has withered leaving long slender compact seed spikes which provide ideal points for smaller arrangements. Use air method No. 1 or No. 3.

P. major rosulatis

This is the cultivated form of plantain which will be well known to all who have visited the gardens of the late Marjory Fish or who know her book *A Flower for Every Day*. The large elongated rosette-shaped seedheads would, I am sure, be an asset to any flower arranger.

HARVESTING AND PRESERVING Although I have not been fortunate enough to be able to prove its preserving qualities, I have included *P. major* as I am confident that its heads would dry by the same method as the wild form. It would also be well worth while experimenting with glycerine method No. 2.

POPPY *see PAPAVER*

RHUS
R. typhina
STAG'S HORN SUMACH

A very handsome shrub or small tree is the North American stag's horn sumach. In America it often grows much taller than in Britain. In late summer the large dense erect seedheads are covered with fine red hairs which gives the complete head its characteristic red velvety texture and flower-like form.

HARVESTING AND PRESERVING Although these seedheads remain on the tree until the following year, they need to be gathered when they are most colourful which is usually late summer to early autumn. Later they gradually lose their colour.

ROSE BAYWILLOW HERB *see CHAEMERION*

RUDBECKIA
CONE FLOWER

There are many forms of this attractive garden plant, some annual but most perennial, all producing large single, yellow, yellow and maroon, or brown and maroon flowers. Although listed as coneflower I am inclined to believe that this name should really be reserved for *R. amplexicaulis* which is a native of Texas, Kansas and Louisiana and has distinctive dark brown cone-shaped centres. Other forms have a flatter rounded centre.

HARVESTING AND PRESERVING Gather as soon as the petals fall and preserve these dark seed discs by air method No. 1 or No. 2. These are most useful when several are wired together in small clusters. Individually they provide ideal centres for 'fun flowers', suggestions for which can be found in my book *The Art of Preserved Flower Arrangement*.

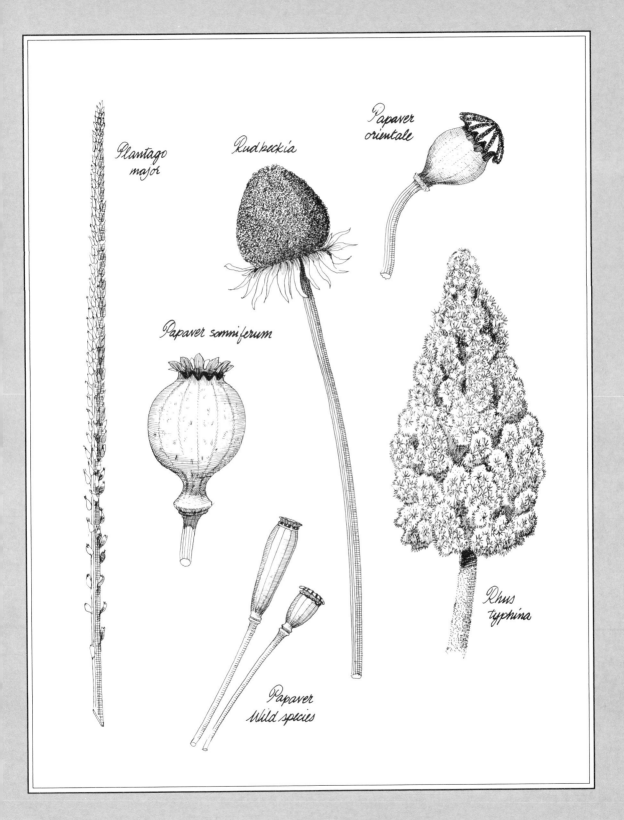

Plantago major

Rudbeckia

Papaver orientale

Papaver somniferum

Papaver Wild species

Rhus typhina

RUMEX
DOCK

During the summer months the common dock can be found growing in many varied situations, being almost as abundant on waste ground in towns as it is in the countryside. The dense plumes of fruiting sepals are highly decorative for arrangements, but there are many varieties and, if you look closely, you will see that some have a more delicate appearance than others, due to the smaller and somewhat looser formation of the sepals.

HARVESTING AND PRESERVING It is possible to preserve dock seedheads from green through shades of red and tan to quite a deep rust shade, by gathering at different stages of growth.

NOTE If left too late the seedheads will easily shed.

SCABIOUS
S. 'Paper Moon'

This hardy annual is an interesting introduction for the flower arranger. It has soft lavender-blue flowers but it is more valuable after its flowers have faded, leaving a decorative sphere of calyces which are already dry and papery.

HARVESTING AND PRESERVING Gather as the flowers are fading. The petals will usually drop out naturally—if not, remove any which persist. The heads are ready for use immediately without any additional drying.

STAG'S HORN SUMACH *see RHUS*

STINKING IRIS *see IRIS FOETIDISSIMA*

ST JOHN'S WORT *see HYPERICUM*

SUMACH *see RHUS*

TEASEL *see DIPSACUS*

THLASPI
T. arvense
FIELD PENNY CRESS

An annual weed of gardens, arable fields and wasteland. Like other species of penny cress this plant produces tiny insignificant white flowers during midsummer. However, unlike the characteristic tiny heart-shaped seedpods produced by other varieties of penny cress, the field penny cress has relatively large heart-shaped seedpods which makes this an extremely decorative weed and one which I am always delighted to find.

HARVESTING AND PRESERVING When the seedpods are fully developed right up the stem, air dry using method No. 1 and No. 2. They will eventually turn a lovely creamy shade.

TRAVELLER'S JOY *see CLEMATIS VITALBA*

TULIPA
TULIP

Tulips belong to the spring, and, regardless of the fact that they do not appeal to me for use in arrangements as out-of-season flowers, and do not even preserve really successfully due to their high moisture content, I have no hesitation in including them in this section. Many of the species produce very striking seedpods. One in particular that I know is *kaufmanniana,* the water lily tulip. Others produce equally attractive seedpods.

HARVESTING AND PRESERVING Gather after the pods have opened and are practically dry on the plant. Use the air method of preserving to ensure the stems are completely dry before use.

UMBELLIFERAE

This is a large group of plants botanically known as Umbelliferae, all of which produce the characteristic umbelliferous-shaped seedheads. Many of these are worth collecting, especially the larger ones, which are also attractive in skeleton form after the seeds have been shed. Their architectural beauty can be seen to advantage in line arrangements rather than in mass. One of the most attractive seedheads, and one which I have come to use frequently, is wild angelica (see page 90).

HARVESTING AND PRESERVING As for wild angelica.

VERBASCUM
V. thapsus
GREAT MULLEIN

Also known as Aaron's rod, this form of wild mullein is a biennial. It has large soft downy leaves which grow in the form of a rosette from which is produced a tall dense inflorescence of yellow flowers. During July and August it is by these flowering spikes, which stand like sentinels on roadsides, rough grassland and waste ground, that this mullein is easily recognisable. The flowering head of the mullein is later followed by a bold spiky seedhead. These are invaluable to provide height in an arrangement.

HARVESTING AND PRESERVING Gather at any time after they are fully mature, but check that each individual seedpod has opened and released its seeds, thus enabling further seedlings of mullein to develop. Dry by air method No. 1 or No. 2.

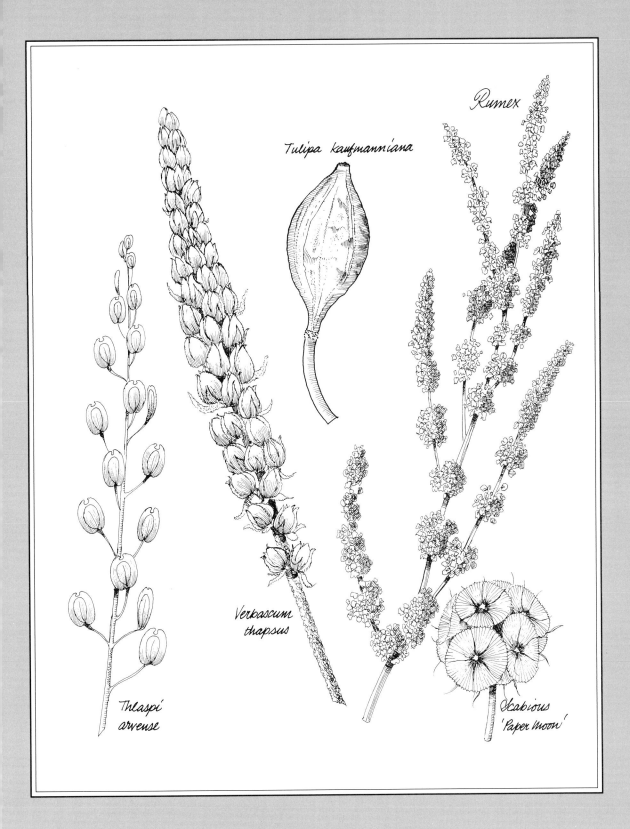

Rumex

Tulipa kaufmanniana

Verbascum thapsus

Thlaspi arvense

Scabious 'Paper Moon'

Pinus ayacahuite

Cones

With one exception, the cones to which I refer are all produced by coniferous trees, most of which are evergreen. They are, in fact, the fruits of the conifer, containing the seeds. When young many are quite soft, but, after fertilisation, the carpels, or scales as they are usually called, become woody and later open to release the ripened seeds. With some conifers this process of growth can take as long as three years. An awareness of the remarkable structure of cones makes us appreciate what a wonderful designer nature is. Their sculptural forms, together with their hard woody texture, likens many of them to intricate wood carvings. The cones illustrated all belong to the following groups of trees. I feel their classification may be helpful when trying to identify other cones of similar structure.

THE PINE FAMILY (PINACEAE)

Spruce, fir, larch, pine and cedar are all members of the pine family (Pinaceae). Their cones, while differing considerably from each other are basically all formed of spirally arranged overlapping scales.

THE CYPRESS FAMILY (CUPRESSACEAE)

The cones of the cypress family differ from those of the pine family. For, instead of consisting of a large number of overlapping scales arranged in a spiral cone, there are often as few as eight scales. The edges of these are at first joined to form an almost globular shape. Later, when the cone is ripe, the scales separate to release the seeds. At this stage of growth, the cones of the cypress take on a completely different form as you will see.

THE SWAMP CYPRESS FAMILY (TAXODIACEAE)

This is an ancient group of trees in which the cone scales are formed by a fusion of both bract and cone scale, which creates the unique sculptured edges of the scales. The two cones which I have included in this section I find particularly decorative: the Californian redwood and the California big tree or wellingtonia.

At a glance it would seem that all cones are brown, which basically, of course, they are, but the variation of shades is considerable, not only among the different species, but depending on the age of the cone, many being lighter when young and becoming darker with maturity. You will also discover that cones that have lain for a considerable length of time on the ground, being continually saturated with rain, are much darker than the ones that have just fallen from the tree.

Much of the interest of cones used in decorative work will lie in the blending of these different shades, so do bear this in mind and try to collect a variety of shades, together with a selection of shapes, from the different species, in various sizes, including some which have opened and some which are still tightly closed.

Many conifers are naturalised in woodlands and forests, making it easy to combine the collecting of their cones with the collecting of nature's many other interesting gifts. However, in order to build up a collection containing as wide a variety as possible of shapes and forms, it becomes necessary to extend our searching to include gardens, country estates, parkland, ancient ruins and even churchyards, for it is here that many of the more unusual cones are to be found. Such trees as the Californian redwood, the Californian big tree (wellingtonia), the Chinese fir and, of course, the cedars were much planted in past centuries as specimen trees for their ornamental value, their architectural forms now contributing so much to the landscape. I am sure, when visiting such places, no one will object to a few *fallen* cones being gathered. Holidays abroad can also provide an excuse to search for yet more different types of cones.

ALDER   *see ALNUS GLUTINOSA*

ALNUS
A. glutinosa
COMMON ALDER

The alder is the one 'cone-bearing' tree I have included which is not coniferous. Although it is widely distributed throughout Britain and Europe, it may possibly not be so well known as many of our conifers.

    The alder is a small moisture-loving deciduous tree and for this reason can be found growing on the banks of streams and rivers, or in other moist places. The 'cones' are smaller than those of most conifers and grow in sprays. These cones ripen in early winter, at which time the scales open to release the seeds, but the empty cones remain attached to the branch, where they continue to hang throughout the winter.

HARVESTING AND PRESERVING   As the male catkins first appear in winter, branches complete with both 'cones' and catkins can be gathered in early February. These are extremely decorative. They can be dried naturally, but tend to become very brittle and the catkins soon break off. I prefer to use the glycerine method No. 1. Individual sprays of cones can just be left to dry naturally. I find both the complete sprays and individual cones ideal to use in association with other cones for arrangements, pictures and plaques.

ARAUCARIA
A. araucana
MONKEY PUZZLE TREE
or CHILEAN PINE

A native of the Chilean Andes and northern Patagonia, the monkey puzzle is only grown in the British Isles under cultivation. Although the monkey puzzle is a cone-bearing conifer, I think it must be better prized for its leaf-covered branches. These leaves are very different from the other foliage described in Chapter 2. In fact, in their dry state, looking rather like the scales of a cone, the overlapping leaves which are pointed and very stiff, entirely cover the branches and so resemble a cone I have decided they should be included under this heading.

HARVESTING AND PRESERVING   Although when growing the leaves are green, we are only concerned with dead branches which can be found under the tree. It is interesting to note that the leaves remain green and functional for ten to fifteen years, after which time it may take several more years for the leaf-covered branches to turn brown and fall, by which time they will be completely dry and permanently preserved.

USES   Should you be fortunate in obtaining a branch or even part of a branch, in a piece it is valuable for modern line arrangements, and cut into individual sections, each resembling a flower, it provides wonderful material for use with cones, etc., in arrangements. Even individual leaves can be used effectively.

CALIFORNIA BIG-TREE   *see SEQUOIADENDRON GIGANTEUM*

CALIFORNIAN REDWOOD   *see SEQUOIA SEMPERVIRENS*

CHAMAECYPARIS
C. lawsoniana
LAWSON CYPRESS

This is the 'false' cypress of which there are now several hundred forms under cultivation. The Lawson cypress is a native of north-west California where it is known as the port-Oxford cypress. These trees are particularly valuable for their dense evergreen foliage (see page 58). Although they are cone-bearing, individually these are too small for use other than in plaques. However, short branches, on which these tiny cones are particularly prolific, can provide decorative plant material for the flower arranger. Either dry naturally using air method No. 1, or, alternatively, use glycerine method No. 1.

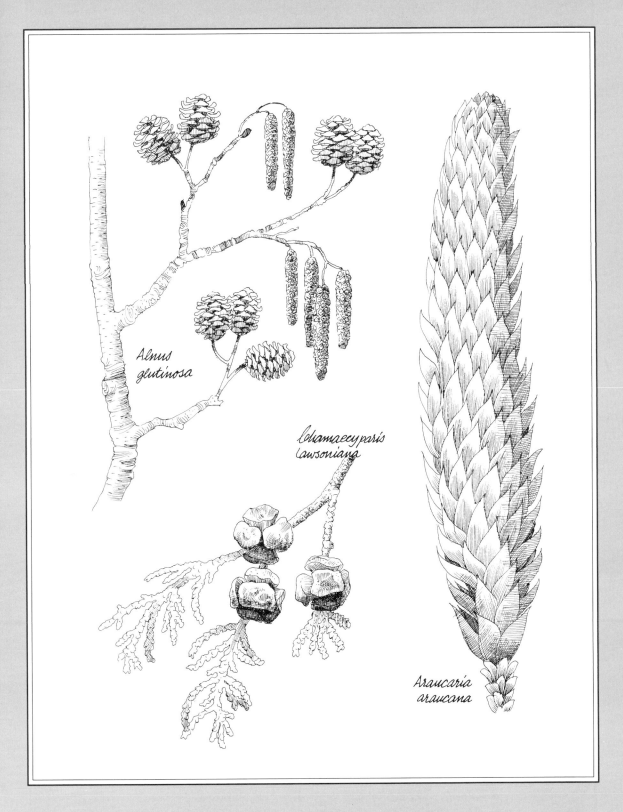

Alnus
glutinosa

Chamaecyparis
Lawsoniana

Araucaria
araucana

CEDRUS
C. libani
CEDAR OF LEBANON

This truly magnificent tree must be familiar to everyone, and in particular those who visit great gardens and stately homes. It is easily recognisable by its broadly rounded or flat-topped crown and its massive horizontally extended branches of foliage. The large barrel-shaped cones of the cedar can only be dried intact if you are lucky enough to obtain some immature cones which have been picked from the tree. When ripe cones break up on the tree to release their seeds, the ground underneath the tree becomes littered with large individual scales. If we look carefully among the scales we can find the centre of the cone which usually remains more or less intact. Their attractive rosette shapes provide us with interesting flower-like forms for arrangements if fixed to a false stem (see page 154). Two trees which are possibly better known to American readers are *C. deodara,* or the Himalayan cedar as it is commonly known, and *C. atlantica,* the Atlantic cedar. These trees also have barrel-shaped cones similar to the cedar of Lebanon. These will also provide the keen-eyed flower arranger with attractive rosette-shaped centres.

CHILEAN PINE

see ARAUCARIA ARAUCANA

CHINESE FIR

see CUNNINGHAMIA LANCEOLATA

CUNNINGHAMIA
C. lanceolata
CHINESE FIR

This is described as moderately hardy and shapely. It is only quite recently that I discovered this tree growing in one of Britain's famous National Trust gardens. I found it very difficult to identify as so many tree books do not show it. From its leafy branches I felt that it could have been a species of araucaria. The cones are extremely decorative and flower-like, in many ways they resemble the Japanese larch but are much larger with a more open form, and each scale having a spiky tip. Their unique habit of falling complete with a long length of stem enables them to be used in arrangements without the need of wiring.

CUPRESSUS
C. lusitanica
MEXICAN CYPRESS

This is one of the many forms of true cypress, and one which is grown in large gardens as an ornamental tree. Its cones are easily recognised by their globular form (see page 111) which in colour are a shiny rich brown. These cones provide a contrast of shape to the many other elongated cones.

C. sempervirens
ITALIAN CYPRESS

A native of Greece and Crete, but commonly planted in the Mediterranean region, this is another form of true cypress grown under cultivation. This cypress bears cones which, in form, are practically identical to those of the Mexican cypress, although in colour they are greyish.

EUROPEAN LARCH

see LARIX DECIDUA

JAPANESE LARCH

see LARIX KAEMPFERI

JAPANESE UMBRELLA PINE

see SCIADOPITYS VERTICILLATA

LARIX
L. decidua
EUROPEAN LARCH

Unlike other coniferous trees, the larch is deciduous. It is a native of the mountains of central Europe and can be found growing in most parts of the British Isles for its timber. Its cones are very attractive, being small and rather egg-shaped. The twigs of the larch are also decorative due to the little knobbly joints which remain after the needles have fallen. These are ideal for use in cone plaques, etc., where they make delightful decorative stems.

L. kaempferi
JAPANESE LARCH

This larch is now extensively cultivated in Britain for its timber. The cones are smaller and more rounded in shape than the cones of the European larch. In fact their dear little rosette shapes make them, I think, the most beautiful of all cones.

MONKEY PUZZLE

see ARAUCARIA ARAUCANA

NORWAY SPRUCE

see PICEA ABIES

PICEA
P. abies
NORWAY SPRUCE

This is one of the older forest trees of Britain and is extensively planted in Europe for its timber which is familiar to us as white deal or white wood. In its young state it is possibly better known as our familiar Christmas tree. The cones of the Norway Spruce are pendulous and practically cylindrical in shape. They reach a length of about 12 cm (5 in), with a $1\frac{1}{2}$ in diameter.

Cedrus libani A

Picea abies

Cunninghamia lanceolata

B

Cupressus lusitanica

Larix decidua

Larix Kaempferi

PINUS	This hardy fast-growing tree from Mexico produces large banana-shaped cones. Although each

PINUS
P. ayacahuite
MEXICAN WHITE PINE

This hardy fast-growing tree from Mexico produces large banana-shaped cones. Although each cone can measure as much as 36 cm (15 in) in length, for their size they are extremely light in weight, making them ideal for large pedestal arrangements. To my delight, I recently discovered this tree growing in a local park. Its cones, however, are not easy to find in large quantities, as, no doubt due to their size and rather striking appearance, after falling they would almost certainly be gathered up by the first person to pass by.

P. peuce
MACEDONIAN PINE

This is a tall stately narrow pyramidal tree of the mountains of Yugoslavia, Albania and western Bulgaria, closely related to the Himalayan blue pine. Both the Macedonian and the Himalayan blue pine produce cones which vary little in form from those of the Mexican pine, but they are shorter and the Himalayan are less curved. All the above named cones are often very resinous, although, with storage, the resin eventually dries and, I feel, adds to the cones' surface texture.

P. pinea
STONE PINE

Being quite the most spectacular cone in my collection I felt its illustration should not be omitted from this section. I list it as a pine due to the formation of its scales. I collected these cones many years ago while visiting the Botanic Gardens on the island of Madeira. At that time I noted its name but this has since escaped me, so I am not absolutely sure that I have identified it correctly. These attractive and extremely decorative large shiny brown cones measure some 10 cm (4 in) across. When open they reveal a dark, almost black, contrasting inner.

P. sylvestris
SCOTS PINE

This is the only native British pine, which, until about 8,000 years ago, formed forests over much of the country. Native pine forests are now confined to the Scottish Highlands. Elsewhere, however, this pine is planted extensively. Its cones, which measure 5–7 cm (2–3 in) in length and ripen in their second year, are familiar to everyone who has ever collected 'fir cones'.

PSEUDOTSUGA
P. menziesii
DOUGLAS FIR

This tall conical tree is a native of North America. A distinctive feature of the cone of this tree is its bract-scales.

SCIADOPITYS
S. verticillata
JAPANESE
UMBRELLA PINE

A native of the mountain areas of Japan, although its common name is umbrella pine, it belongs to the swamp cypress family, Taxodiaceae, due, I imagine, to the form of the cone scales. It is a tree which is not often seen under cultivation in the British Isles, but I have included it because its medium-size light-weight cones are so attractive. I must confess that I have only recently been able to add some of these cones to my collection, but the sheer delight of finding them makes the looking so worthwhile.

SCOTS PINE *see PINUS SYLVESTRIS*

SEQUOIA
S. sempervirens
CALIFORNIAN
REDWOOD

Considered to be the tallest tree in the world, this native of California and Oregon has frequently been planted as a specimen tree in parks and gardens in the British Isles. For such a large tree I am always amazed at the relatively small size of its cones which measure only 2–2.5 cm ($\frac{3}{4}$–1 in) in length.

SEQUOIADENDRON
S. giganteum
CALIFORNIAN
BIG-TREE or
WELLINGTONIA

This majestic tree is probably the largest, although not the tallest, tree in the world. A native of the Californian mountain region, this tree is found in large parks and gardens where it is planted for ornamental purposes. The cones of the big tree are of medium size and are particularly interesting in form and texture.

STONE PINE *see PINUS PINEA*

TSUGA
T. heterophylla
WESTERN HEMLOCK

This tall narrowly conical tree, which is planted for its timber, is a native of North America. Its tiny pendulous cones are smaller than those of most other conifers; in fact they are among the few cones that are suitable for miniatures.

WELLINGTONIA *see SEQUOIADENDRON GIGANTEUM*

WESTERN HEMLOCK *see TSUGA HETEROPHYLLA*

Pseudotsuga menziesii

Tsuga
heterophylla

Pinus
ayacahuite

Sciadopitys
verticillata

Pinus
sylvestris

Sequoiadendron
giganteum

Sequoia
sempervirens

Pinus peuce

Pinus pinea

Hard fruits, nuts and succulent berries

There are many fruits, both hard and succulent, which can be successfully dried for use in flower arrangements: these not only provide colour or textural interest, but the necessary contrast of form which is so often needed to make an arrangement just that little bit different. Therefore, in this section I include hard fruits, which I feel cannot be adequately described as seedheads, and also certain succulent berries for which I feel the following information may be helpful.

SUCCULENT BERRIES
The fruits of many shrubs and plants consist of seeds contained within succulent berries. As these develop and ripen, many become brightly coloured. With few exceptions their preservation at this stage is generally not successful. In spite of the application of various lacquers I find that most berries gathered when fully mature will slowly become shrivelled. My experiments with berries have shown that many will respond to being gathered in their fully developed green state and allowed to continue their process of ripening in an arrangement. Treated in this way, I have often kept autumn berries throughout the winter, particularly black bryony. On the other hand, even shrivelled berries can sometimes be beautiful (see mahonia). I sometimes even find the odd occasion when nature has had more success than I have with drying berries such as *Hypericum elatum,* which, as a result I have been able to keep for several years.

AESCULUS
A. hippocastanum
HORSE CHESTNUT
Although I have not had the occasion to try these, I am sure that, in early autumn, short leafless branches of prickly green fruitcases, containing the familiar conkers, would respond to being treated in the same way as branches of beech nuts, and produce equally satisfactory results.

BEECH *see FAGUS*

BLACK BRYONY *see TAMUS*

COLYLUS
C. avellana
HAZEL
On page 22 I have described the flowering catkins of the hazel. In this section I refer to the fruits of the same tree, which, when ripe, are well known to us as hazel nuts. There may be little need to preserve these for their decorative value, but, for a special purpose, small branches could provide an interesting feature in an arrangement.

HARVESTING AND PRESERVING Gather branches of hazel nuts before the nuts become ripe and fall. The green nuts, together with their frilly green 'cups', will preserve successfully by glycerine method No. 1. After this treatment the nuts will stay tightly nestled within their leafy cups.

GOURDS
Gourds belong to the same family as the vegetable marrow, the pumpkin and the squash, and are grown in the same way. The plant will ramble over the ground or up a trellis, producing small hard fruits which are used purely for decorative purposes. The fruits vary enormously, both in shape, colour and texture: they can be round, egg-shaped, pear-shaped or even bottle-shaped, green, yellow or orange, or sometimes a mixture of all three colours, striped, mottled or plain. Then again, some are smooth-skinned, while others have a surface which is covered with a curious wart-like growth.

HARVESTING AND PRESERVING It is important that gourds should be completely ripe before harvesting. One is best able to judge this by the deepened colour of the fruit, and the hardness of their skins, which, when tapped, should sound as hard as wood. If you are still in doubt as to whether or not they are ripe, it is better to leave them a few days longer, rather than gather them unripe which will result in mildew. Cut the gourds from the plant on a dry day, leaving a piece of stem attached. This will be useful if you are later wiring them for use in arrangements. Handle them very carefully to avoid bruising, and dry them in a warm place—an airing cupboard is ideal. When they have completely dried out, they should have a somewhat hollow sound when tapped. The treatment of dried gourds is a matter of personal choice. They can be left completely natural, or, if desired, can be given an application of clear varnish, either gloss or matt. Personally I prefer to polish them with a natural-colour wax polish.

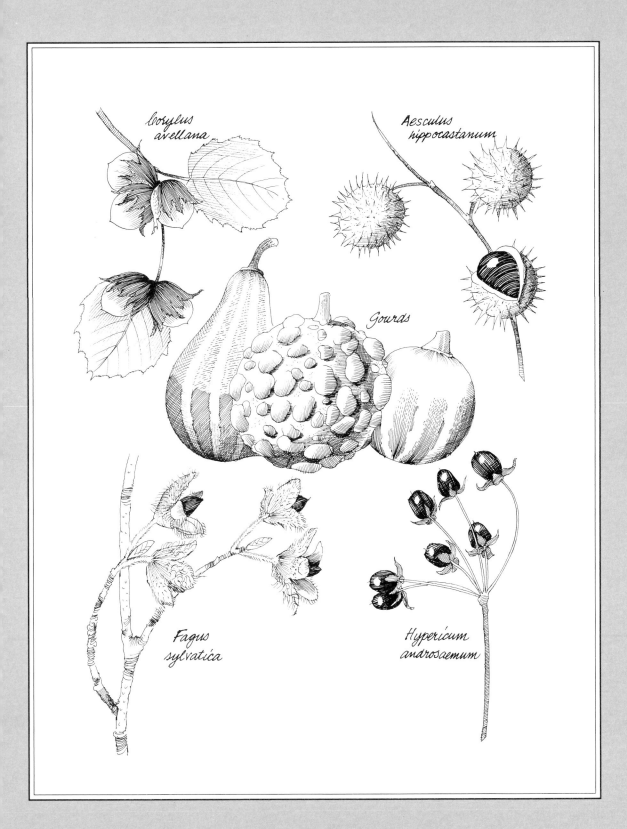

Corylus
avellana

Aesculus
hippocastanum

Gourds

Fagus
sylvatica

Hypericum
androsaemum

FAGUS
F. sylvatica
COMMON BEECH

The beech tree provides one of the most popular foliages for preserving, details of which can be found on page 64. In this section I have included the fruit of the beech, often referred to as beechmast. It consists of a green outer case which contains two nuts. As it ripens it becomes woody with a very rough surface. When the nuts are ripe, this fruitcase splits open into four petal-like forms and the ripe nuts fall out, revealing the beautifully smooth inner surface of the case.

HARVESTING AND PRESERVING While branches of these empty seedcases are very decorative, I prefer to collect those on which the fruitcases are still green and remain tightly closed. If these are preserved using glycerine method No. 1, the cases will open, but the nuts will remain firmly anchored. Branches preserved in this way will also remain supple instead of becoming brittle.

NOTE If desired, the leaves can be left on the branches, for they, of course, will also preserve. However, I usually find it more satisfactory to preserve separate non-nut-bearing branches of leaves and therefore I strip the nut-bearing ones of their leaves before preserving them.

HAZEL NUTS *see CORYLUS*

HORSE CHESTNUT *see AESCULUS*

HYPERICUM
H. androsaemum
TUTSEN

This shrubby perennial is smaller-flowered and generally more common than most hypericums, and in many parts of Britain it can be found growing wild. In its fresh state I find it attractive at all stages of growth, but particularly when its immature berries are surrounded by bright green flower-like bracts. These preserve well by the desiccant method, and, used individually, are ideal for miniature arrangements. When fully developed and ripe these berries turn almost black. If left in the garden until early winter or even later, I find that, providing the season has not been excessively wet, the berries will have dried naturally without shrivelling. A light brushing of clear varnish will enhance the surface of these berries, giving them a jewel-like quality.

LIME *see TILIA*

MAHONIA
M. aquifolium

These berries can be dried in the same way as *M. japonica,* but their colouring is not so attractive and the berries grow in clusters which I find are not so useful.

M. japonica

During the grey days of winter I always welcome the beautiful flowers of the *Mahonia japonica,* but they are flowers to enjoy for their delightful perfume, for they have little value when preserved. However, in the spring, as the flowers fade, long sprays of small greyish-green berries develop. As these ripen they turn an almost metallic slate-blue colour and develop a grape-like bloom.

HARVESTING AND PRESERVING Gather as soon as the berries begin to turn colour. This is most important, because if you do not pick them, the blackbirds will! I have often lost a whole season's berries in this way. Dry the berries by the air method. Although they will shrivel when dry, I find it is not so apparent as in many other berries because the beautiful grape-like bloom is retained. For more impact, wire several stems together.

MAIZE *see ZEA MAYS*

PHYTOLACCA
P. decandra
POKE WEED

Often referred to as red-ink plant, the poke weed grows in North America. The small white flowers, which are not at all showy, are borne in racemes; these are followed by large green berries, which, when ripe, turn deep purple, each one resembling a small hard black berry. These fruits are ornamental but not edible.

HARVESTING AND PRESERVING At their unripe green stage, these berries will dry by air method No. 1, when they will retain most of their green colouring and provide an unusual and interesting form for arrangements.

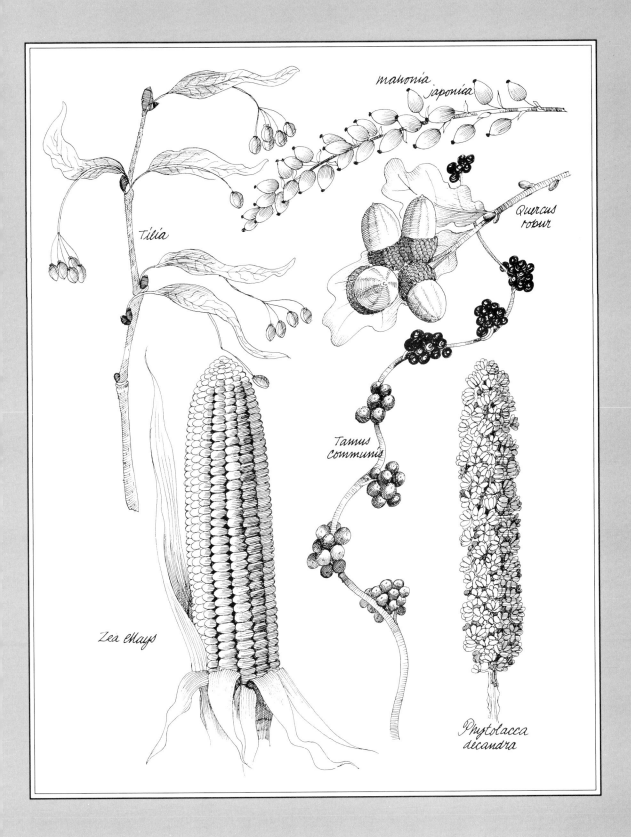

mahonia japonica

Tilia

Quercus robur

Tamus communis

Zea Mays

Phytolacca decandra

POKE WEED   *see PHYTOLACCA*

QUERCUS   The shiny green acorn in its little green cup is one of the familiar sights of the autumn countryside,
Q. robur   but, as autumn advances, the acorns turn brown and fall.
COMMON OAK

HARVESTING AND PRESERVING   Gather branches of unripe green acorns, complete with
their cups, and preserve using glycerine method No. 1. When preserved the nuts should remain
intact. If by chance one or two ripen and fall out, a blob of glue on the base of the acorn will soon
secure it again. Like the beech, these branches may also be preserved with or without their leaves.

TAMUS   This wild perennial climbing plant is found mainly in hedgerows, but it also grows on scrub land
T. communis   and on the edge of woods. During the summer months its insignificant flowers, on long twining
BLACK BRYONY   stems, are inconspicuous amongst the luxuriant hedgerow growth, but, as autumn approaches,
clusters of large shiny green succulent berries form, which later turn bright scarlet. These are
extremely attractive and showy, but, for drying, they must be gathered while still green and allowed
to ripen either by hanging to dry or while in an arrangement. Treated in this way I have been
able to keep them through the winter. One word of warning—do keep them away from children,
if eaten they are **poisonous**.

TILIA   There are several species of lime in general cultivation, and of these *T. vulgaris,* the common or
LIME   striped lime, is the one most widely planted. I find that lime foliage is generally too soft, and not
even particularly decorative, to use in flower arranging, but the fruits of the lime are extremely
decorative. They grow in clusters, with a strap-shaped bract attached to the stem.

HARVESTING AND PRESERVING   It is important to wait until late summer when the hard
fruits have grown to full size, which is about the size of a small pea. By this time the bracts will
be fully developed. Select branches which have well-formed bracts and fruits, strip off the leaves
and preserve by glycerine method No. 1.

NOTE   The preserved branches of bracted fruits are often referred to as striped lime.

TUTSAN   *see HYPERICUM*

ZEA   Botanically this plant should be included in the section on grasses, but as it is so unlike any other
Z. mays   grass, I feel it provides a more useful reference in this section. In America this annual plant is
MAIZE   referred to just as corn. It is very different from any other known plant. It is unknown in the wild
and I have been unsuccessful in finding its country of origin, although apparently it could be from
South America. There are several kinds of maize, but the one with which we are most familiar is
the golden sweet corn, often referred to as corn-on-the-cob. The maize cob consists of an axis
with the fruits attached. These are protected by large overlapping bracts. There are several
ornamental varieties of maize which produce kernels or rather fruits of many colours, including
brown, mahogany and slate-blue, 'Multicoloured Pierrot' and 'Indian Corn', being two such
varieties.

HARVESTING AND PRESERVING   Gather the cob when the corn is ripe. Remove the silky
tassel from the tip of the cob, this being the remains of the terminal male inflorescence. Remove the
outer bracts, but I would suggest leaving at least some of the inner bracts. This must be a matter
of preference, but, certainly for large arrangements, they provide interest if just turned back to
expose the cob. If all the bracts are removed, I feel the form of the corn cob in itself has a rather
solid form. Dry the cob in a warm place, if possible in an upright position.

5 NON-FLOWERING PLANTS

Ferns, Mosses, Fungi, and Lichen

I have grouped these four families of plants together, as I feel they differ so much from the other plants which are referred to in this book. Although they do not resemble each other in appearance, they all have several characteristics in common. Ferns, mosses, fungi and lichen are the most primitive forms of plant life on this planet, and, unlike other plants, they produce no flowers and therefore no seeds. Reproduction among the species of each family is by means of spores.

To many people possibly little may be known of such plants as fungi and lichen, not only of their habitation and how they grow, but also of their decorative value when preserved. To try and create a better understanding of these curious and yet fascinating non-flowering plants, I have written a few basic facts about each family.

Ferns

In flower arranging, ferns are usually grouped together with leaves, and classed under the heading of foliage. However, in nature they are a group apart, and belong to the family of non-flowering plants known as Filicales. It is this reason, and also the fact that many species are naturalised, making them readily available, that has made me decide to deal with them under their own heading.

As ferns are non-flowering plants, they reproduce themselves by spores. Fern spores are dust-like and contained in capsules called sporangia. They are found on the underside of the fern's leafy part, in the form of small brown, or sometimes almost black, patches. This leafy part of the fern can vary enormously in the different species, both in form and texture. Take, for instance, the tough and leathery strap-shaped leaf of the hart's tongue fern, and then, in contrast, see the lacy frond of the lady fern, its frond completely divided into small leafy portions, each single portion in itself resembling a beautiful little fern in miniature.

The frond of the fern, as we usually refer to it, consists of the leaf blade and its stalk. In the spring the fronds of some of our more common deciduous ferns (for example, the male fern), are both beautiful and curious, as the illustration shows. They rise from the plant looking rather like a bishop's crozier and, as they unfurl, many are clothed in thin brown chaffy scales. If we capture their beauty at this stage by preserving them, they will add a special interest to an arrangement when used with the mature fronds which we can gather and preserve later in the season. A few are evergreen and can be gathered even during the winter, but, as spring awakens, even the evergreen ferns will produce new fronds which, until fully mature, will usually be too soft to retain their shape when preserved.

It must be remembered that the ferns described in the following pages are only a few of the many species to be found growing in woodlands and hedgerows. However, I have tried to include ferns which differ from each other not only in shape and form, but also in size and texture. This I hope will make it possible for readers to look for other species with similar characteristics, with a view to preserving them, including the many cultivated varieties which are becoming increasingly popular as they enjoy a revival from the Victorian era, particularly as pot plants.

WHERE TO FIND WILD FERNS

One usually associates ferns with damp shady places, but this can really only be said of some of the species, for others grow in dry walls, while the common bracken will be found on open heathland exposed to sun, often with little moisture. To help you in your search for the different species, I have given, with each one, a description of its natural habitat.

WAYS OF PRE-SERVING FERNS

I have dealt with the preservation of a few species under their individual headings, in particular those for which preservation is possible at various stages of growth. With regard to ferns in general, most can be preserved in one of two ways, either by using glycerine method No. 2, or the desiccant method. If using the former, the fronds must be mature but still green. However, I find the desiccant method invaluable for use if the ferns are not completely mature, or when difficulty is experienced in getting the ferns to absorb the glycerine mixture. In autumn, as the fronds of the bracken fern begin to die, they develop beautiful autumnal colourings of cream, yellow, gold and brown. By using the desiccant method, we are able to capture these colourings, and also to retain the ferns' natural form, which I feel is preferable to the old method of preserving them under the carpet, which, of course, renders them completely flat.

STORAGE

Keep in boxes away from light, for use as required.

ADIANTUM
A. capillus-veneris
MAIDENHAIR FERN

The fronds of maidenhair fern are indeed very graceful. Although this is one of Britain's native ferns, it is now very rarely to be found growing wild, but is commonly cultivated as a pot plant. Each individual leafy portion of this fern is in the shape of a fan, and, although it appears too delicate for preserving, its wiry stems make it, in fact, one of the most satisfactory species. Use either the glycerine method of preservation which will produce a beautiful olive shade, or the desiccant method which will retain the fern's greenness. The required colour will possibly be the deciding factor as to which method is chosen. When preserved, each frond can also be divided into smaller sprays.

ASPLENIUM
A. ruta-muraria
WALL RUE
SPLEENWORT

You will notice that the wall rue spleenwort does in fact resemble the leaves of the garden rue, which is probably how it gets its name. This pretty little fern is common throughout Britain and can be found growing on both limestone walls and on the mortar of brick walls. It is one of our smallest ferns. The fronds, which first appear in May or June, measure only an inch or two when fully mature. This fern has a very tough texture and the laciness of the fronds, together with its size, makes it an ideal choice of foliage for miniature arrangements.

A. trichomanes
MAIDENHAIR
SPLEENWORT

This fern is naturally a limestone plant, but can be found growing in the crevices of old walls throughout Britain. As one of our more common ferns, it is sometimes referred to as the common wall spleenwort. Although the fronds of this graceful fern can vary considerably in length, depending on its habitation, I have never found them to exceed more than a few inches. Being an evergreen fern, it can be preserved at any time of the year.

PRESERVING Due to their size it is of little advantage to try to preserve either of these ferns by the glycerine method, especially as the desiccant method preserves them exceptionally well.

ATHYRIUM
A. filix-femina
LADY FERN

Found growing in moist places throughout the British Isles, the lady fern deserves its name as it is one of the most beautiful of our larger ferns.
    The fronds of this fern shrivel completely with the autumn frosts, but, if the shrivelled mass is carefully moved to one side, one is able to observe solid reddish brown scaly lumps. These lumps are the new fronds ready to unfurl in April or May, at which time, if we are lucky, we may capture them during their various stages of unfurling, complete with chaffy scales.

PRESERVATION The crosier-like shapes of these new fronds can be preserved by the desiccant method. Mature fronds gathered later will respond to the glycerine method, but can also be preserved by the desiccant method.

BLECHNUM
B. spicant
HARD FERN

This fern can be found throughout Britain, but not on calcareous soil. In the south and east of England it grows in moist places in woodlands and also on the shady banks of open ditches. In the wetter north, however, it is to be found on open heath and also in the clefts of exposed rocks.
    It is a most useful and satisfactory fern for preserving, for, as the name implies it has tough fronds which retain their firmness when preserved. This fern can easily be identified because of the two types of fronds, both of which are produced on the same plant, one being the fertile frond of erect habit. By far the more decorative, however, are the barren fronds which have a spreading

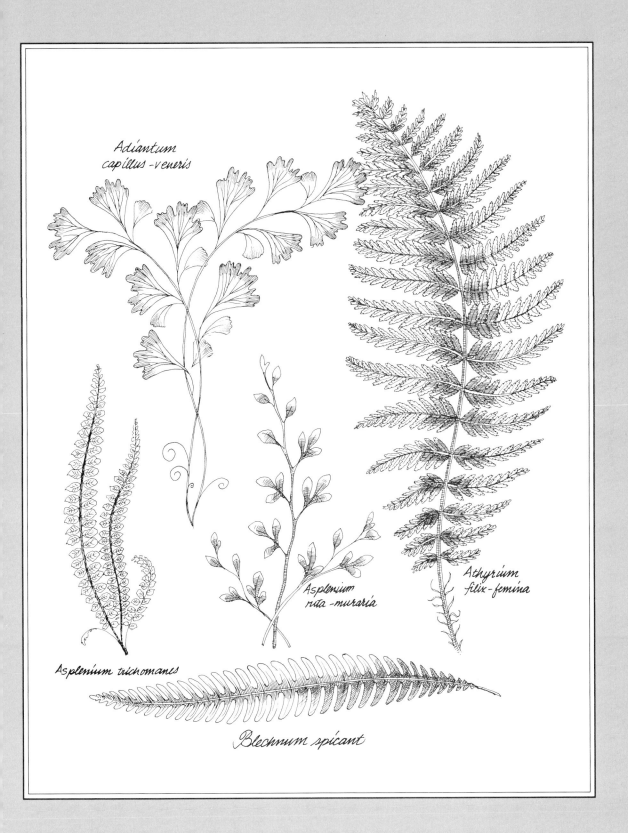

Adiantum capillus-veneris

Asplenium ruta-muraria

Athyrium filix-femina

Asplenium trichomanes

Blechnum spicant

habit, often being quite prostrate. Both types are illustrated, but I would recommend collecting the barren ones which can be preserved at any stage of growth depending on their intended use. The really tiny fronds, which are usually found on young plants, can measure as little as 5 cm (2 in) and are ideal for miniature arrangements. They can also be used in woodland scenes where several, grouped together, can be tucked between moss, wood or fungi in such a way as to create the impression of actually growing.

The larger fronds are very versatile and can be used in association with a variety of preserved materials, in many types of arrangements.

BRACKEN FERN   *see PTERIDIUM*

COMMON POLYPODY   *see POLYPODIUM*

HARD FERN   *see BLECHNUM*

HART'S TONGUE FERN   *see PHYLLITIS*

LADY FERN   *see ATHYRIUM*

MAIDENHAIR FERN   *see ADIANTUM*

PHYLLITIS
P. scolopendrium
HART'S TONGUE FERN

Although the hart's tongue fern can be found throughout the British Isles, it often only grows in localised areas. Shady banks in woodlands, or the moist banks of ditches in country lanes are among the most likely places to look, particularly in the south and west of Britain. This fern, in itself, is possibly not as decorative as the other species I have mentioned, but I felt it should be included as the fronds differ so greatly in appearance from those of most other ferns. They are tough, solid and strap-shaped, and can provide excellent material for preserved line arrangements. Make sure you gather the fronds in various sizes, as they can be found growing from between 30–60 cm (1–2 ft) in length.

POLYPODIUM
P. vulgare
COMMON POLYPODY

This is an evergreen fern which can be found, at any time of the year, growing in the leaf mould of old hedgerows, or that which has gathered between the root-limbs of old oak trees. It is also to be found growing out of the masonry of old walls where it roots in the accumulated humus which has formed from the growth of mosses. Common polypody can be found throughout Britain. It can easily be recognised by the oval shape of its fronds which are tough and leathery and can vary in length from a few inches to 45 cm (18 in) or often more, depending on the conditions under which it is growing.

POLYSTICHUM
P. setiferum
SOFT SHIELD FERN

This is a most elegant and graceful fern. The entire stem of *P. setiferum* is covered in soft brown chaffy scales, while, in contrast, the finely divided fronds give this fern a beautiful lacy quality which makes it my favourite of all the larger ferns. It also has the added bonus of retaining its fronds throughout the winter, provided it is planted in a sheltered place. This is one of the few ferns in which the growth of the mature fronds is horizontal, and for this reason I like to plant it overhanging stones which helps to protect the fronds from becoming bedraggled during the winter months.

HARVESTING AND PRESERVING Gather completely formed undamaged fronds at any time of the year, although the contrast in colour between stem and frond is far greater in early summer when the fronds are bright green and the scales a rich reddish brown. Preserve using the desiccant method.

PTERIDIUM
P. aquilinum
BRACKEN FERN

I am sure this fern requires no introduction, for it can be found growing in abundance almost anywhere. It must have been used by practically everyone at some time or other in connection with floral work. Nevertheless, I feel that such a fern cannot be omitted from this chapter, as maybe not everyone realises all its possibilities.

To many people this fern will be referred to as just bracken, and not in any way associated with the family of ferns. Let us take a look at the fronds when they first appear in May, each rising from its stout creeping rhizome in the form of a shepherd's crook. It is well worth while capturing their beauty at this stage by gathering a few for preservation by the desiccant method. After this stage of growth the fronds will be of no further use for preserving until they reach maturity in about August, for when the fronds first unfurl they are too limp, if preserved, to be of any real value. From August onwards we can gather the fronds while they remain green and preserve them using either the glycerine or desiccant method. It is unlikely that sucess will be achieved with the

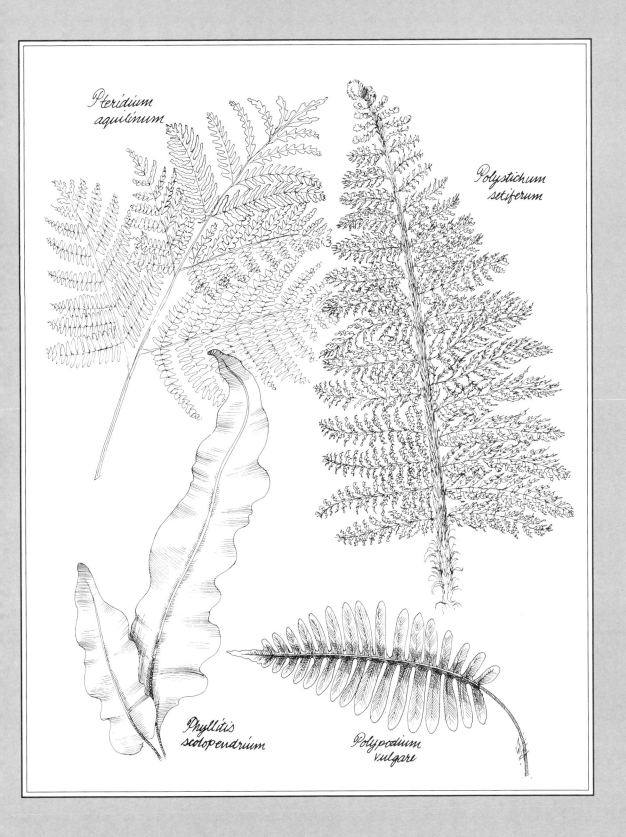

Pteridium aquilinum

Polystichum setiferum

Phyllitis scolopendrium

Polypodium vulgare

former unless each stem is first divided into individual fronds. Later in the season, before the fronds begin to curl from early frosts, complete stems of bracken fern, or individual fronds, can be found in shades ranging from creamy white through to beautiful golds. At this stage, desiccant preserving will be the only suitable method. If, after preservation, during either the green or the golden stage, the bracken fern is twice divided, each tiny leafy portion will be found to resemble a complete fern in itself, these being ideal for use in miniature arrangements.

SOFT SHIELD FERN *see POLYSTICHUM SETIFERUM*

WALL RUE SPLEENWORT *see ASPLENIUM*

Mosses

To many people moss is classified as a weed which grows in abundance on lawns and is difficult to irradicate. But moss, like other so-called weeds, is really only referred to as such when it is found growing where it is not wanted. Mosses belong to the group of non-flowering plants known as Bryophyta, and reproduce themselves in the same way as ferns, by means of spores. Each plant consists of a stem and leaves and has root-like rhizoids which attach it to its substratum. At all seasons of the year, mosses can be found growing in a variety of situations, but are most abundant where the air is free from excessive smoke pollution. Generally speaking, the surrounding air needs to be relatively humid for mosses to flourish. This is possibly why a large number of species are found in shady conditions. Although it is not essentially the shade they require, such places generally hold more moisture, thus creating a higher humidity which is important to the luxuriance of their growth. Another point to bear in mind when searching for mosses, regardless of the species and their habitat, is that they will generally be found where other vegetation is relatively sparse.

A closer look at some of these fascinating little plants, of which there are about 600 species in Britain, will be found to prove most rewarding, but I hasten to add that many are microscopic and therefore do not concern us, and that even many of the larger species will not retain their original shape sufficiently well when preserved to be of any great value in decorative work. The following descriptions of some of the species, together with a few ideas as to their uses will, I hope, act as a guide to the types of mosses to look for.

THE COLLECTING AND PRESERVING OF MOSSES Gather them while moist at any time of the year, weather permitting. Their colours are found to be richer under moist conditions. If gathered during a drought, most mosses will be dull and dingy; for example, the cushions of white fork moss will be a dirty white colour. I would advise using a knife to sever mosses from their substratum. This will ensure that they are kept intact, but do be extremely careful in handling them, as, while they are still full of moisture, they will break up very easily. The preservation of mosses is a very simple operation, but first we must clean them, i.e. remove any debris, leaves, twigs, or clinging earth, etc. Having done this, lie them upside down on sheets of absorbent paper (newspaper will do). Leave them in a convenient dry place away from direct light and where air can circulate freely. A change of paper after a short time may be necessary. If gathered and dried in this way, the mosses' natural colours will be retained. The time of drying will vary according to the type of moss and amount of moisture present. As a general guide, a few days is usually long enough for the feather mosses and the other fine-textured ones, but it may take a few weeks before the cushion mosses are completely dry.

STORAGE Kept in boxes away from light, they will last indefinitely, for use as required.

IDEAS FOR USE As these species of moss are so often associated with wood in their natural habitat, I like to use them in connection with wood or fungi in arrangements. To cover completely an interesting-shaped branch by fixing moss to it with clear adhesive makes an interesting feature in an arrangement, or, alternatively, it can be used as a foundation for a woodland or hedgerow arrangement. These are only a few suggestions for using these species of moss. If you keep a supply at hand, you will find endless uses for it. It can be used as fresh moss again just by soaking the required amount of moss in water for a short while. The water will be quickly absorbed by the moss which will regain its fresh appearance. This is particularly useful during the winter months when frost or snow makes it impossible to gather moss, and also during periods of drought when fresh moss has lost its greenness. It can also be a great boon to the town dweller who has limited access to fresh moss.

A GUIDE TO ᴇCIES WHICH DO NOT PRESERVE WELL

It is, I am afraid, impossible to make a sweeping statement about which mosses are of no decorative use when preserved, but the ones I have found to be unsuitable are many of the bog and peat mosses which grow under very wet conditions. These species are able to absorb much water, and, when this is extracted, I find their leaves shrivel and remain clinging to their stems, looking rather as dead leaves on the stems of flowering plants do. Therefore, if, after collecting and preserving a particular species, you are not happy with the result, do not accept this as applying to mosses in general, but try other species instead. I can assure you that not only will you find many that are extremely useful and decorative, you will also receive much pleasure from studying each tiny stem of leaves from the many species.

Cushion type mosses

**GRIMMIA
G. pulvinata
GREY CUSHION MOSS**

This moss is usually found growing on wall tops, stone windowsills and roofs. It has characteristic pretty little round cushions but, due to their subdued dark greenish-grey colouring, they are certainly not as conspicuous as the moss described below.

**LEUCOBRYUM
L. glaucum
WHITE FORK MOSS**

To a non-botanist like myself the name white fork moss seems inappropriate for this delightful rich green moss. I can only imagine that it refers to the colour of the growing moss during a period of drought when it is a dirty white, and that, botanically, it has a forked branched structure which is not readily apparent and would need to be seen with the aid of a magnifying glass.

This conspicuous and decorative moss is said to grow in pine, birch and beech woods where the soil is poor and acid. Living in an area renowned for its beech woods, it is only here that I have ever found this moss. Its common name of bun moss aptly describes its characteristic habit of growth, which is in the form of very compact green cushion-type mounds or hummocks. These can be so tiny that I have used them in miniature arrangements, but an average size is 15 cm (6 in) in diameter. In Germany I once found some which were enormous, both in diameter and depth. Having found an area in which this type of moss grows, gather it sparingly, leaving the site as undisturbed as possible, so that others who pass that way, and who are able to appreciate its beauty, may have the pleasure of seeing these beautiful little green cushions in their natural habitat.

FEATHER MOSS

To many people feather mosses may pass unnoticed, accepted as just moss, but to find them we must first develop a seeing eye. Even then, feather mosses may not always be easy to find, but the search can often be well rewarded, for, when preserved, they retain their characteristic feather or fern-like form. They really do resemble exquisite little feather-like ferns. The identification of the different species of feather mosses must be left for the botanist, as the characteristics appear to vary only slightly between many of them.

MAT-FORMING MOSSES

There are many species of moss which, for purely decorative reasons, I will describe as mat-forming, as they grow to form dense turf-like mats. Those which grow in abundance in moist places are the ones I like to collect, as, apart from during drought conditions, these usually provide the most vivid green colouring. Vast areas of ground, decaying trees and tree stumps can often be found completely covered in these rich velvety green carpets of mosses. You may be lucky and find interesting pieces of moss-covered wood which can be dried and used as a base for your arrangement, if not I feel it is essential to dry large quantities of this moss to cover bases for woodland scenes and to provide a substitute for fresh moss.

Fungi

Although fungi belong to the vegetable kingdom, the fundamental difference between this form of plant life and other forms I have referred to for preserving, is the total absence of chlorophyll (or green colouring matter) which enables the plant, in the presence of sunlight, to manufacture the organic compounds it requires. Fungi have to obtain their organic food ready made, and some species are found to do this by utilising dead or decaying plant material, in which case they are said to be seprophytic, while other species attack living plant material and are therefore parasitic.

A characteristic of the fungi, also common with ferns, mosses and lichens, is that they reproduce themselves by spores, and not by seeds as most other plants do. There are about 6,000 species of fungi in Britain, and it is not possible for me to give a complete list of which to preserve and which not to. However, I hope the following guidance will help with which types are satisfactory to preserve for use in floral or decorative work, thus preventing the rather slimy smelly mess that has at times been my misfortune to encounter through experiments carried out with unsuitable types. I have also given brief notes as to the time of year to search for fungi, their habitation and how to preserve them.

BRACKET FUNGI The characteristics of these fungi are the extremely tough and leathery, corky, or sometimes even woody, textures. They are bracket-shaped and grow on trees, tree stumps, or fallen branches, and are generally to be found at any time of the year.

You will most likely be attracted to the fungi within this group by their beautiful zones of colour, which vary in the different species from white and cream through to the many shades of brown. Sometimes, with age, their upper surface develops a beautiful green colouring. This is caused by the growth of microscopic algae. However, in no way does this prevent them from being preserved, but instead adds to their charm when used in arrangements. You will discover many species of these bracket fungi have a surface just like velvet.

All species within this group are suitable for preservation. Once preserved, these will keep indefinitely, and are invaluable, not only for combining with other preserved materials in arrangements, but often as accessories or bases. Here I have mentioned only those which I personally have found to be the most decorative, and which are also generally found to be among the more common species. There are several species of bracket fungi which, although they are very hard and woody and dry exceptionally well, are too large to be of any real value in floral work. However, if you are lucky enough to find any of these, they can, when preserved, make an interesting feature displayed in a conservatory, together with unusual pieces of wood.

The species of bracket fungi to which I refer are usually of the perennial kind which means they continue from season to season, building up layer upon layer of spores. This, of course, is the reason they became so large. To find fungi of this type we must search at the bases of old trees.

PRESERVING BRACKET FUNGI Due to their characteristically hard texture, most bracket fungi will dry naturally if laid on absorbent paper in a dry place. However, if, after gathering these fungi, they are required for immediate use, it is possible to dry them quickly by placing them in the oven at a temperature not exceeding 200°F, and leaving them until all the moisture has dried out and they are quite hard. In this rather quick drying process, I have found the larger types, such as *Trametes gibbosa*, may warp slightly, but often to their advantage I may add, for not only will they often develop interesting shapes, but the one I tried by this method warped just enough to enable it to become self-supporting for use as a base.

Some of the more solid types of hoof-shaped bracket fungi, such as *Polyporus belulinus,* are more satisfactory when preserved by the borax method. They may take as long as three weeks before they are really hard and dry, but I think it is the only safe way to preserve them, for, due to the thickness of the flesh, if left to dry naturally, mould will often develop before the drying process is completed, and also the edges, which are thinner, have a tendency to curl.

TREATMENT OF BRACKET FUNGI TO DESTROY INSECTS Bracket fungi occasionally become the homes of many tiny unwelcome creatures, although these may not be visible when we gather the fungi. But do not despair, for, if any are noticed after the fungi are preserved, they can easily be dealt with using methylated spirits. The clear methylated spirits is ideal, being free from colouring, but, as this can only be obtained by permit, it is not usually readily available. Instead, we must use the coloured domestic kind sold in hardware shops. This is quite satisfactory if diluted and used in the following way.

METHOD Mix one part methylated spirits with one part water, and soak the fungi with this mixture. This can be done either by standing them in it for a few minutes, or by flopping the mixture over the fungi with a paint brush. The latter is the more practical way when dealing with large fungi as far less methylated solution will be required. This treatment may not kill any eggs that are present, and it may therefore be necessary to repeat the process again later if more insects appear.

If desired, this treatment can be used as a precautionary measure when the fungi are first gathered, although, as they only occasionally harbour bugs, I personally would rather wait and hope that none appear, especially with the fungi which have a velvety texture, as, after soaking, the velvety effect becomes less apparent.

PUFF-BALL AND MUSHROOM-TYPE FUNGI Although bracket fungi are the easier and most useful to preserve, many other species are worth searching for and experimenting with, for although they may not be of use as bases, they can indeed create interest and arouse curiosity when used in a woodland arrangement, or even just embedded in a setting of dried moss.

The fungi I now refer to are the toadstools, puff-balls, etc. Unlike the bracket fungi, most appear and disappear as quickly as a flower, and, just as flowers have their particular season for blooming, individual species of fungi are also only to be found at certain times of the year. Although a few species of these annual fungi are found in the spring, I think it to our advantage if we concentrate on the time of year when the majority are to be found, this being in late summer and during autumn, with the months of September and October producing by far the greatest variety.

PRESERVING PUFF BALLS AND MUSHROOM-TYPE FUNGI As puff-balls are usually most abundant after rain, they will naturally be very wet unless they have had time to dry off. This being so, I would suggest severing them very carefully from their substratum, using a sharp knife, and then keeping them spread out in the natural warmth of a room for several hours.

I have only had success with preserving these using the borax method, as, if the surface is wet, borax will adhere to it.

The species which have stalks must be placed in the borax upside down, with the stalks uppermost. It is not necessary to cover the stalks completely with borax, but the caps must have at least 1 cm ($\frac{1}{2}$ in) over them.

There are a few points worth remembering when deciding whether or not species of fungi you find are suitable for preservation. For, without doubt, if you once develop the seeing eye and begin looking, you will find many more different species from these I have mentioned, many of which you will be able to preserve equally well.

1. Avoid any specimens with slimy caps.

2. Avoid species of the genus Lactarius which, when cut, will produce a milky substance.

Fungi which fall into either of these two groups generally result in a rather smelly mess if you try preserving them.

The *Observer's Book of Common Fungi* is very useful for further information on fungi, and has many illustrations which can be a great help when trying to identify species.

DAEDALEA
D. quercina

This species of fungi is common on oak stumps. It is hard and bracket-shaped, or may possibly be referred to as hoof-shaped. It differs from trametes and polystictus, being thicker and the upper surface smoother. Although zoned, these zones are less conspicuous, in shades of light brown, and sometimes, when young, I have even found them in a beautiful honey colour. When you sever these fungi from their substratum and turn them over, you will observe the large elongated wavy tubes which are rather open and very deep. The flesh is very corky in texture, and a greyish-beige colour.

SUGGESTIONS FOR USE I often feel this species is as decorative, or possibly more so, when used upside down, but this of course is a matter of choice. However, I have used them both ways, and often in a similar manner to trametes and polystictus. They could also be built up in tiers round an interesting piece of wood, the wood, of course, being used vertically.

HYGROPHOROPSIS
H. aurantiaca
FALSE CHANTERELLE

This fungus is often called *Clitocybe aurantiaca* and is found in conifer woods and on heaths in late summer. Its rich orange funnel-shaped form is very distinctive and therefore easily seen as it contrasts with the dark brown earthy floor of the woodland. Under the cap this fungus has the characteristic gills of many of the mushroom-type fungi, but their somewhat dry texture is an indication that it is suitable for preserving.

LYCOPERDON
L. perlatum
PUFF BALL

These curious, rather solid-looking fungi are most frequently found in conifer woods, usually found growing in little groups, quite close to each other. When young, they are a greyish-white, but develop a more yellowish-fawn colour as they rapidly mature. It is for their interesting form and their wart-like texture, rather than their beauty, that I find these fungi so valuable. If you find a group, it is usually possible to gather varying sizes, from tiny immature ones to the larger balls nearing maturity. Avoid fully mature ones, for they are inclined either to go soft when preserved, or to explode to release their spores.

MORCHELLA
M. esculenta
MOREL

Unfortunately this is a fungus which I have had no success in finding. However, I am including it because I feel sure it would preserve successfully. It occurs in the spring, and can be found in clearings in woods and hedgerows. The colour varies from yellow-ochre to a brownish shade, and the texture of its head is not unlike a honeycomb, as you will see from the drawing.

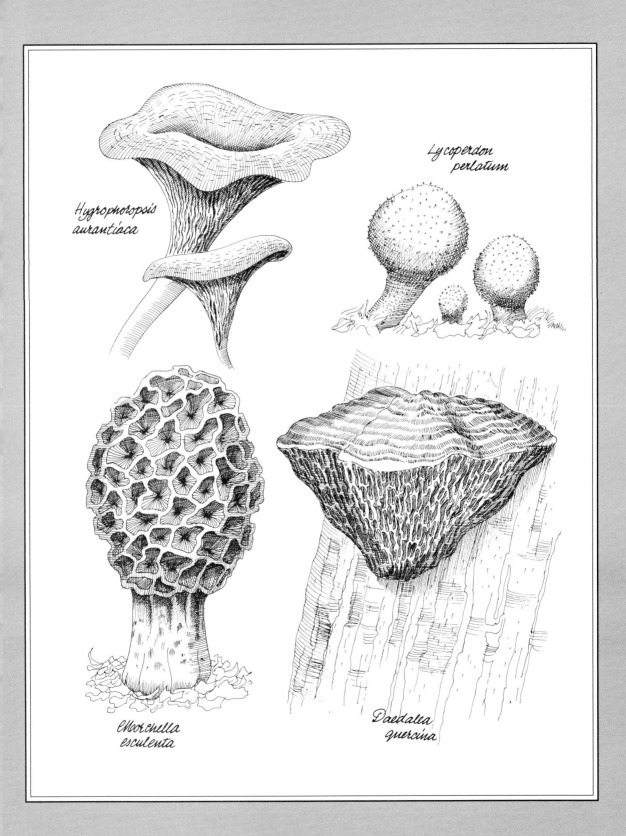

Hygrophoropsis aurantiaca

Lycoperdon perlatum

Morchella esculenta

Daedalea quercina

POLYPORUS
P. belulinus

These bracket fungi are to be found on the dead trunks of birch trees where they are usually very conspicuous. They are possibly not as decorative as the bracket fungi previously mentioned, due to their rather solid appearance. When fully grown, these fungi are somewhat hoof-shaped, with a smooth greyish-brown upper surface formed by a distinct skin. The flesh is extremely thick and of a corky texture. It is ideal for use in large arrangements.

POLYSTICTUS
P. versicolor

Possibly the most common of the bracket fungi, this species is to be found at any time of the year, growing on old stumps, fallen logs and branches. The characteristics are similar to *Trametes gibbosa*, but the zones of colour are more distinctive and the brackets are thinner and leathery, as opposed to the woody texture of trametes, and I have never found them growing to the sizes that trametes often reaches.

SUGGESTIONS FOR USE As the word bracket implies, these fungi are always found growing as illustrated, and for this reason I feel, when dried, they must be used in a similar way. To stand them on edge, as I have on many occasions seen them used, I think would look very unnatural. If built up in tiers and mounted on a base, they can be made to look similar to my group of trametes, but smaller and more dainty in appearance. I would therefore suggest that the plant materials used with them should also be smaller. Alternatively, I have used them stuck to the side of an interesting piece of wood, giving the impression that they are growing from it, as they do in their natural habitat. We can, I think, learn a great deal about how to arrange many plant materials, particularly the non-flowering ones, simply by observing the way we see them growing.

RUSSULA

This is a genus of fungi of which there are many species. They are conspicuous plants of the woodland floor in late summer and autumn, as they are usually brightly coloured, with caps of scarlet, crimson, yellow, green and mauve. While some of these are most successful when preserved, others lose their colour completely. I regret to say it must be a matter of trial and error, but one thing is certain, they all have the characteristic dryish gills which enable their shape and form to preserve successfully.

SCLERODERMA
S. aurantium
COMMON EARTH BALL

This is one of our more common fungi which may be found in late summer, autumn and early winter, frequently on heaths and often in areas where birch trees grow. It has no stem, is rather bun-shaped and is usually of an ochre-yellow colour with a wart-like surface similar to the puff ball. Like the puff-ball this fungus can also be found in groups of various sizes, but, again, avoid the really mature ones in which the gleba (the inside) has become powdery. These are inclined to split easily.

This is another fungus which I consider to be curious and interesting, rather than beautiful.

TRAMETES
T. gibbosa

This fungus is to be found on the stumps of deciduous trees throughout the year, often forming extensive patches with brackets arranged in tiers. If you are lucky, as I have been, to sever carefully a whole group from the stump, keeping it intact, you have a ready made base.

SUGGESTIONS FOR USE After preserving, a hole can be made in which to conceal a container to take your plant materials. I think, however, that as a group of these fungi have such an interesting form and beautiful velvety texture, there should be restraint in the addition of other plant material. If moss is used, care should be taken not to cover the beautiful zones of colour. These can vary from olive green to grey, or often a brownish-black, and are so characteristic of this species.

Scleroderma aurantium

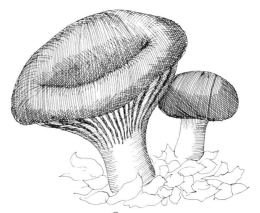

Russula

*Polyporus
betulinus*

Polystictus versicolor

Lichen

Lichen could be referred to as a dual plant, as it consists of two quite different organisms growing together in intimate association—a fungus and a microscopic green plant called an alga, each supplying some need of the other. Usually, the fungus makes up the bulk of the thallus, and the algal cells are buried within it. This makes the lichen differ from true fungi in as much as the algae contain chlorophyll and therefore manufacture their own food which both the fungal component and the algae live on. The alga manufactures carbohydrates which are also used by the fungus. By the continuous renewal of both the fungal element and the algal element, the lichen can live almost indefinitely, and, for this reason, can be found at any season of the year. Although they can endure extremes of cold and heat, dryness and moisture, they do, however, prefer a moist climate. Lichen are very sensitive to atmospheric pollution and therefore few will grow near industrial towns. I have found them to be abundant in the South West of England, especially near the sea.

The characteristics of most lichen are a greyish, sometimes yellow, network of filaments. According to the species, they grow on walls, rocks, trees and old decaying tree stumps. I find lichens fascinating and beautiful little plants. Although I have only included a very small selection of the several hundred lichens which can be found, there are others which are similar in form and equally useful for their unique decorative qualities. There are, of course, many which are extremely decorative, but which grow so closely and firmly to their substratum that it is impossible to remove them.

DRYING LICHEN

Lichens require no special treatment other than the removal of any debris that may have collected among the filaments. They should be spread out on a sheet of paper in a cool, dry, airy place and left until all the moisture has dried out, or, in the case of a lichen-covered branch, leave it standing in a container until both branch and lichen have dried out. They can then be kept indefinitely in boxes and used as required.

BEARD LICHEN

see USNEA

CLADONIA
C. rangiferina
REINDEER MOSS

This is the true reindeer moss. Although so-called, it is botanically a lichen. It is characteristic of Arctic areas where, I believe, it is the food of reindeer, hence its name. In Britain it is said to grow mainly on the high Scottish moors. The characteristics of this particular lichen are the grey branched growth which forms intricate rather coarse sponge or moss-like masses. There are other species of cladonia which are more widespread and occur abundantly on heaths, moors and bogs, etc. To my delight, I have found them growing in profusion amongst heather on the Isles of Scilly.

HYPOGYMNIA
H. physodes syn. Parmelia
physodes

This is one of the most common lichens. Its characteristics are that the grey-green thalus forms elegant rosettes. Although it grows on rocks also, it is possibly more useful to the flower arranger when it is found growing on trees. If a carefully selected lichen-covered branch is used in an arrangement, restraint in the use of other plant material is necessary to prevent the beauty of the branch being lost. Should you not be lucky enough to find the exact shaped branch to suit your requirements, it is possible to cheat a little by carefully cutting off branches that are growing in the wrong direction and, using a contact glue, attaching other branches to give the required shape. If this is done with care, the joins in the improvised branch can be covered by sticking on extra rosettes of lichen.

REINDEER MOSS

see CLADONIA

USNEA
U. articulata
BEARD LICHEN

This is one of the largest and most conspicuous of British lichen, which grows mainly on old trees but occasionally on rocks and is especially abundant in the west. I have found some good specimens on rocks in the Isles of Scilly. Sometimes complete trees can be seen covered with this hoary type of grey-green lichen which I can only describe as growing in long bearded filigree formations which hang free from rock or branch. It is very difficult to remove these lichen intact as they are very firmly attached to their substratum. If found growing on branches, a complete branch could be selected to use as a feature in a large arrangement, otherwise I find it is possible to sever them with a sharp knife.

6 METHODS OF DRYING AND PRESERVING

While it is necessary to understand fully the different methods before attempting to dry or preserve any type of plant material, the real secret of success depends on applying the right method to the right material. Each method has its own particular use and, with few exceptions, one method cannot be used instead of another to produce the same results from identical materials. Colour, texture and form are necessary ingredients of all types of preserved work, and, unless full use is made of the three main methods, work in this field is limited.

AIR DRYING

Air drying is the simplest of all methods, requiring the minimum of time and no special equipment. This is a great boon to those of us who are too busy to experiment with other techniques, and also to the beginner who has not attempted preserved work before, because quite interesting arrangements can be made with air-dried materials alone. Materials suitable for drying by this method are as follows:

bracts (see page 9);
cultivated grasses (see page 76);
wild grasses, (see page 80);
seedheads (see page 87);
foliage (Cupressus) (see page 58);
everlasting flowers (see page 45).
See also the selection of flowers from Chapter 1.

Most other flowers will not dry successfully by this method, due to the formation, size or texture of their petals.

At one time I would have considered air drying to be completely covered by one method, but, through time and many experiments, I have proved myself wrong. This is probably mainly due to the wide and varied range of materials for which this method is suited.

If air drying is to be used successfully and to its best advantage, it must be subdivided into four sections, although each conforms to the same basic principle. This is of course, as the very words 'air drying' imply, that moisture is removed from the materials by the circulation of air, without the aid of any form of preservative. As neither complicated nor time-consuming methods are required for air drying, there is a great temptation to gather large quantities of one type of plant material, for instance seedheads. This is fine if they are all needed, but arrangers who are drying for their own pleasure are well advised to be selective and gather small quantities of a wider variety of plant materials, concentrating all the time on contrasting shapes, forms and textures.

The two golden rules for plant materials gathered for air drying are the same for the glycerine and desiccant methods of preserving.

1. Make quite sure that the plant materials are free from moisture, such as rain or dew.

2. Select only materials in perfect condition, as imperfections show to an even greater extent in preserved work than in fresh.

PREPARATION OF PLANT MATERIALS

See the details given with individual plant materials for the ideal stage of growth at which they should be gathered. Sort through the plant materials and discard any that are damaged or malformed. Any leaves attached to the stems will need to be removed as, even if they are still fresh and green, they will become too shrivelled and brittle to be of any use. Large leaves that come away easily should be removed at this stage, but smaller leaves will break away much more easily after they have dried when, in fact, really tiny ones will just rub off.

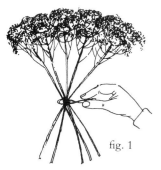

fig. 1

AIR DRYING METHOD No. 1

Gather the plant materials into small bunches and secure them with plastic-covered wires (fig. 1). As the stems dry and shrink these can be tightened much more easily than string. I have discovered that plastic-covered wires sold as garden ties are the perfect length for this purpose; alternatively, freezer-bag ties can be used. Hang bunches, heads down, in any convenient place which will comply with the following conditions: *cool, dry, airy* and *dark* (fig. 2). The latter, if necessary, can be achieved by the use of a dust sheet suspended to exclude the light (remembering that north light will bleach the colour from your materials as much as sunlight). Do not encase your materials in the dust sheet, as it is essential for air to circulate to absorb the plants' natural moisture, and, after all, dried material is only natural material that has been encouraged to dehydrate.

NOTE Plant materials of a pendulous nature, in particular many species of grasses, are more successful if dried by method No. 2 which will retain or encourage this feature.

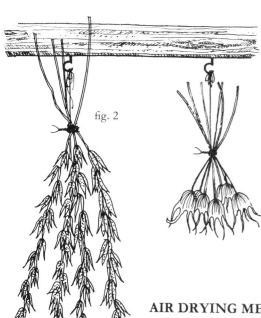

fig. 2

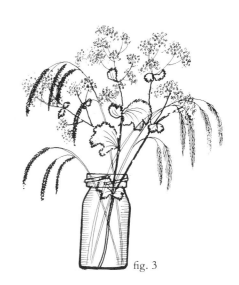

fig. 3

AIR DRYING METHOD No. 2

I find the plant materials that benefit from being dried by this method, in preference to method No. 1 are mainly as follows:

cultivated grasses with a pendulous nature (see page 76);
wild grasses with a pendulous nature (see page 80);
seedheads with a pendulous nature (see page 87).

Other plant materials, referred to in method No. 1, can be successfully dried by this method as an alternative if suitable hanging space is not available, providing they have sufficiently firm stems. Plant materials are stood in an upright container (fig. 3) in the same conditions as method No. 1.

AIR DRYING METHOD No. 3

Plant materials, according to type, are either hung in small bunches, heads down as for method No. 1, or, alternatively, stood in an upright container as for method No. 2, the only difference being the conditions under which they are dried—*warm, airy* and *dark*. This method is often useful for flowers which are suitable for air drying, particularly during periods of excessively damp weather conditions, or if space is not available under the previously stated conditions.

AIR DRYING METHOD No. 4

I really like to refer to this as the 'arrange and dry method' which I find particularly successful for some calyces and just a few flowers, these being: hydrangeas, molucella or erica.

NOTE Successful results can only be ensured if calyces are completely mature and feel really firm to the touch. Recut the stems and immediately stand them in about 12 mm (1 in) of water (fig. 4). Allow them to take up this water and then dry out. No further water should be added. I must emphasise that hydrangeas and molucella in particular have to be fully mature to enable them to be preserved successfully by this method. If picked too early, the calyces will still be soft and will curl or shrivel up; they will in fact just look 'dead'. I try to leave them growing until quite late in the autumn, only gathering them before the first hard frost destroys them.

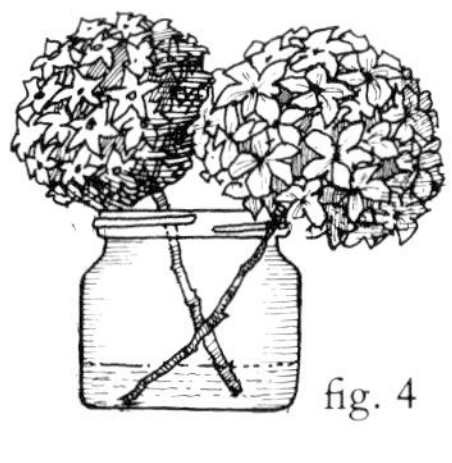

NOTE For molucella I only suggest this as an alternative to glycerine method No. 2 which will render the calyces less brittle and ensure they do not easily break away from the stem if constant handling is necessary.

fig. 4

GLYCERINE PRESERVING

For many people, this method of preserving seems to produce unnecessary failure. I feel rather sad about this because it really is so easy once a few basic principles are understood. There will always be the unexplained failure, but this is inevitable in all things, least of all glycerine preserving. Plant materials which respond to this method of preserving include:

    calyces (see page 9);
    evergreen and deciduous foliage (see page 51);
    seedheads (see page 87);
    grasses (see page 74).

CALYCES

I find the glycerine method a particularly successful way to preserve many of the calyces described in Chapter 1. The exception being flowers in which the calyces consist of petal-like sepals which are brightly coloured, hydrangeas for example. It is of the utmost importance that calyces should be mature before they are treated in this way. A common fault is to try to preserve immature calyces, particularly molucella (bells of Ireland), which will go limp and fail to retain its form successfully. When the complete stem of flower-like calyces are mature, each one will be firm to the touch. It may, however, be necessary, even so, to cut out the immature tip of each spike after preserving, as, in cooler climates, the spikes rarely mature to the very tip.

SEEDHEADS

Although seedheads of all types will dry naturally by the air method, some are inclined to become very brittle while others may easily shatter, these usually being plumes of seeds such as wild dock. For these the glycerine method is a more suitable method to adopt as it renders seedheads more supple and therefore easier to handle, and also keeps seeds intact. Bearded seedheads, such as *Anemone pulsatilla* and clematis, will develop a beautiful silken sheen if preserved by this method. It should be remembered that, for successful results, seedheads should be picked before they are fully mature.

FOLIAGE

The flower arranger should make full use of this method of preserving mature deciduous foliage and, in particular, evergreen foliage which, with few exceptions, will not preserve successfully by other methods. Immature deciduous foliage, autumn leaves and some firm-textured herbaceous foliage can be preserved by the desiccant method. The advantage of glycerine-preserved foliage is that it will remain beautifully supple and pliable.

WHEN TO GATHER FOLIAGE

DECIDUOUS FOLIAGE OF TREES AND SHRUBS

To enable us to be successful with preserving deciduous foliage, we must first understand a little about the growth of the tree itself. When the leaves first unfurl they are very tender and will not be sufficiently firm to preserve. However, I think our main concern is with foliage gathered in the autumn, as all too often it is not until this time of the year that many of us think of preserving deciduous foliage.

    I am sure the greatest percentage of failures are due to gathering foliage that has already begun to show autumnal tints. At this stage of growth the sap stops rising and the chlorophyll flows back from the leaf into the twig (chlorophyll being the green matter which gives the leaf its colour) and so the colours of autumn begin to appear and slowly the leaf withers and eventually falls, or shall we say is forced off by little studs of hard cork which form and help to break the cohesion between the leaf stalk and the twig. For this reason, foliage gathered in this condition is unlikely to preserve because if sap is not reaching the leaves, water and glycerine most definitely will not. This means we must gather our foliage when it is mature, from about the end of June through the summer season till autumn, and then, providing we see no sign of colour change in the leaf, successful results should be assured when the glycerine method is used to preserve deciduous foliage.

EVERGREEN FOLIAGE

It is possible to preserve this at almost any time of the year, weather conditions permitting, but remember that most evergreen trees and shrubs produce new leaves in late spring and, although these may not be as tender as those of deciduous trees and shrubs, they will not have developed their true character and texture until they reach maturity later in the summer.

GRASSES

This includes both the wild and cultivated species as described in Chapter 3. If grasses are to be preserved by this method, they must be gathered at the stage of growth when they are just bursting into flower. With most wild grasses this will be early summer, but with cultivated grasses it may be later, depending if they are from self-sown seedlings or have been grown from seed sown in the current year. Once grasses have matured, released their seeds and become dry and hay-like, they will, of course, fail to absorb the glycerine mixture. It may be as well to remember that most green grasses preserved by this method will lose their greenness and become golden, but they will remain very supple. For successful results in preserving pampas grasses by this method it will be necessary to gather them in late summer or early autumn, just as they are bursting from their sheath.

PLANT MATERIALS NOT SUITABLE FOR GLYCERINE PRESERVATION

Here I refer mainly to flowers which, with the exception of catkins, are not satisfactorily preserved in this way, due to the effect the glycerine has on them. Some I have experimented with will not even absorb the mixture and, while many will, I find the results very disappointing: admittedly the flower remains beautifully supple, but its natural colour is completely lost, and one is left with a creamy or fawn-coloured flower.

ADVANTAGES OF GLYCERINE PRESERVING

Unlike other methods glycerine preserving enables plant materials to retain the beautiful supple quality of their fresh counterparts. Most plant materials preserved in this way will either darken or change colour completely, and even materials that only darken when first preserved often change colour completely after a period of time, either during use or in storage. This, to me, is one of the aspects of preserving that makes it so interesting, particularly as it extends the range of colourings in plant materials.

WHAT IS GLYCERINE?

Glycerine is a colourless and odourless syrupy liquid which, when diluted with water, becomes clear and readily absorbed by plant material. It can be purchased from chemists' shops, drug stores and, often, floral art suppliers. Flower arrangement societies also sometimes stock it on their sales tables.

WHY NOT SUBSTITUTE ANTI-FREEZE FOR GLYCERINE?

I am often asked about the use of anti-freeze for preserving. Personally I prefer to use glycerine, but, yes, anti-freeze is suitable although only if it is glycerine-based. Follow the method for glycerine preserving, but do not dilute the anti-freeze. The colours of foliage preserved in anti-freeze can be expected to differ from those of glycerine-preserved foliage, but, after all, it is fun to experiment.

GLYCERINE METHOD No. 1

FOR WOODY-STEMMED FOLIAGE

NOTE Individual soft stemmed leaves should be preserved by Method No. 2.

When you gather branches of foliage for preserving, do not cut them at random. Look at each branch carefully and select only those of a suitable shape for the type of arrangement you are intending to create. Make sure the leaves are in good condition. Remember the golden rules.

1. Make quite sure that your selected foliage is free from surface moisture, such as rain or dew.
2. Select only foliage in perfect condition, as imperfections show to a greater extent in dried and preserved work than in fresh.

In addition to these two points I would desist from gathering any type of foliage during a particularly hot period of the day. Check cut foliage and trim away any damaged leaves and unwanted cross twigs. Thin out areas where the leaves are overcrowded.

PREPARING THE MIXTURE

fig. 5

Add one part of glycerine to two parts of hot water (fig. 5) and mix them together well until the mixture looks clear. Glycerine is heavier than water, and, unless you mix thoroughly, the glycerine will remain at the bottom and only the water will be taken up by the foliage.

Pour the mixture, to a depth of about 75 mm (3 in), into a container which is just large enough to take the foliage. For support, stand this container inside a larger container, such as a bucket, which is heavy enough to prevent the foliage toppling it over (fig. 6). Woody-stemmed foliage should be split (fig. 7) and put into the hot mixture immediately after cutting. During a delay of even five minutes, the base of the stem will seal over and will need to be re-cut to ensure an effective intake of the mixture. I feel sure that a delay between cutting and putting the foliage into the mixture is often the cause of failure when preserving by this method. I find that another common mistake is to stand foliage in plain water for a period of time, allowing it to become so charged with water that the rapid intake of glycerine mixture necessary to ensure successful preserving will not be possible. This is a natural mistake for flower arrangers to make, as, if foliage is to last well when it is used fresh in an arrangement, it must, of course, be conditioned with water.

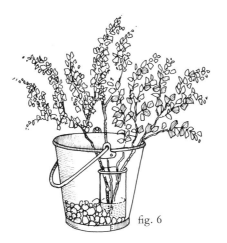

fig. 6

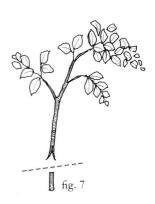

fig. 7

COMPLETING THE PRESERVING PROCESS

Leave your container of foliage to stand in a warm, dry place, away from direct light. In recent years I have discovered that foliage will take up the glycerine mixture more successfully in a warm atmosphere than under cool conditions.

The time taken to preserve leaves varies according to several important factors.

First, the texture and thickness of the leaves. Naturally, thin-textured leaves require less time to preserve than thicker ones.

Secondly, the temperature of the surrounding environment. The mixture is taken up more quickly in a warm room than a cool one.

Thirdly, the time of year and even the time of day that the foliage is gathered often seems to make a difference as to how quickly or slowly it takes up the mixture. Thin-textured leaves, such as cotoneaster and escallonia, will usually be ready in about four days, while tough, leathery leaves, such as elaeagnus or laurel, may take three to four weeks. Foliage will take much longer to preserve in winter than in summer.

Experience will enable the reader to give the foliage enough mixture in the initial stage of preserving to complete the process with maybe a little left over, but the beginner should check the level of the mixture daily and top up with more mixture if necessary.

REMOVING THE FOLIAGE

It is interesting to watch the glycerine mixture travelling through the leaves and observe the gradual change of colour. As an experiment, try removing some evergreen foliage when the mixture has been only partially taken through the leaves.

They may not remain quite so supple, but you will experience some interesting variations of leaf shadings.

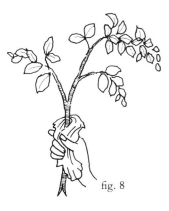

fig. 8

Be sure to wipe the stems dry as soon as the plant materials are removed from the glycerine mixture (fig. 8). A common fault in the unsuccessful use of the glycerine method is to over-glycerine. Foliage requires the intake of only sufficient mixture to retain its supple texture and prevent the leaves from becoming shrivelled. Too much glycerine will result in the leaves feeling oily, often with tiny droplets of mixture visible on the surface of each leaf which can also encourage mildew to form. If this happens, remove your foliage immediately, give it a good swish in warm soapy water, rinse, shake off the excess water and stand it in a warm place to dry.

A NOTE ON ECONOMY

Many people are tempted to throw away left-over glycerine mixture which is very wasteful. It may have become discoloured, but I find that this does not affect its preserving qualities. Strain it through a fine sieve to remove any debris, or even lumps of mould. (Mould will occasionally develop on the surface if the mixture has been allowed to stand for some time after use.) Reheat the mixture when it is needed and use it as before.

HOW TO CONTROL THE FINAL SHADE OF FOLIAGE

SHADES OF GREEN

It is possible to keep the green colouring of some foliage providing that later, during storage and also when used in arrangements, it is kept away from direct light. While in the glycerine mixture, daily inspection is essential and the leaves must be removed as soon as they have absorbed just enough mixture to preserve them. This is usually after a period of four to five days for soft deciduous leaves, such as beech (but longer for tougher leaves), when they will feel soft and silky to the touch, and have taken on a slightly darker shade of green. It is a good idea to have a branch nearby, standing in water alone, to compare the difference in colour and texture.

SHADES OF BROWN

Various shades of brown can be obtained by gathering foliage at different times. Some foliage, such as escallonia, will immediately turn dark brown (in fact almost black) as soon as it begins to absorb the mixture, which means it is therefore impossible to preserve such foliage in its green state.

SHADES OF CREAM

It is possible to obtain beautiful cream shades from many foliages, particularly herbaceous forms. This is achieved simply by exposing the material to strong sunlight during the process of preserving.

These are only intended as guidelines to show the possible results this method of preserving has to offer. For individual foliage, a certain amount of experimenting will be necessary.

SPECIAL AFTERCARE TREATMENT FOR EVERGREEN FOLIAGE

I think that the foliage of evergreen shrubs and trees is the most useful for preserving by the glycerine method because it will keep almost indefinitely, but leaves, such as mahonia and elaeagnus, which have large flat surfaces can look rather drab.

Because of the long growing period of these leaves, the accumulation of dust and grime on the surface of mature leaves can be quite considerable, and this is even more noticeable after preserving, giving the leaves a dull lifeless appearance. However, after cleaning with a spot of oil they immediately become bright, gleaming and fresh-looking. The difference in appearance could be likened to the difference between a polished and an unpolished piece of furniture.

I find that practically any clear liquid oil is suitable for this purpose. For most people the obvious and most accessible oil will be cooking oil from the kitchen. Apply just a spot of oil to a clean soft cloth and wipe over the entire surface of each leaf (fig. 9). Now wipe over the surface of each leaf again, using a clean dry part of the cloth; if necessary repeat this process, until all the oily residue is removed and the leaves feel quite dry. Wiping with oil is also an ideal way of reviving preserved leaves that have been in store for a long time.

fig. 9

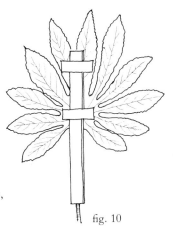

fig. 10

GLYCERINE METHOD No. 2

FOR CALYCES, SEEDHEADS AND GRASSES

Prepare the mixture in the same way as described for method No. 1, but allow it to cool. Recut the stems of the calyces, seedheads or grasses and stand them in the liquid. It is usually only necessary to allow these plant materials to drink the mixture for twenty-four to forty-eight hours, just long enough to secure the calyces or seeds firmly on the stem. Under certain conditions, however, it may be necessary to extend this time. (Read carefully the second part of method No. 1.) When plant materials are removed, do remember to wipe the stems dry.

FOR HERBACEOUS FOLIAGE AND SOFT STEMMED LEAVES OF TREES AND SHRUBS

Use the same mixture and in the same way as described above, but it will be necessary to allow time for the mixture to travel through the leaves, depending on conditions (see the second part of method No. 1). Under warm conditions a week or so will usually be adequate.

SPECIAL AIDS TO SUPPORT INDIVIDUAL LEAVES

During the preserving process, large individual leaves, such as fatsia leaves, have a tendency to flop at the point where the leaf joins the stem and this restricts absorption of the glycerine mixture. With leaves like this, it is a good idea to support the joint with a stick secured to the centre of the leaf and stalk with pieces of adhesive tape (fig. 10). Alternatively, you can use the tape to form a collar round the cupped leaf (fig. 11). The leaf can then be placed lower down in the container so that the rim of the container supports it.

fig. 11

STORAGE OF ALL GLYCERINE-PRESERVED PLANT MATERIALS

Although glycerine-preserved plant materials must be kept dry during storage, it is not advisable to enclose them completely. With a quantity of glycerine-preserved materials a certain amount of moisture is present, particularly if the intake of glycerine has been excessive. For this reason, plastic or polythene bags and boxes should not be used. If the place in which the plant materials are stored is subject to marked temperature changes, condensation may develop on the inside of the plastic and mildew will quickly form. Such conditions are often experienced in attics, which, for many people, are the obvious, if not the only, storage space.

Ideal containers for glycerined foliage are the cardboard boxes in which florists receive their fresh-flower orders; these usually have holes in the sides which will allow air to circulate freely. As these boxes are usually discarded, florists are often more than willing to give them away. Alternatively, any strong cardboard box in which holes can be cut is quite suitable. Glycerined seedheads and calyces, particularly molucella, will become squashed if they are kept in boxes and should either be hung up or stood in jam jars.

Most glycerine-preserved foliage will last for a long time, in fact evergreen leaves, which have a firmer texture than deciduous ones, will keep for many years. However, if storage conditions are particularly hot and dry, the glycerine present in some thin-textured deciduous foliage, such as beech leaves, may dry out, causing the leaves to shrivel.

DESICCANT PRESERVING

Plant materials which respond to this method of preserving include:

    flowers (see details with individual flowers, Chapter 1);

    leaves (immature, autumn and herbaceous, see Chapter 2);

    ferns;

    fungi;

    mosses (to preserve the form of some species).

WHAT IS A DESICCANT?

A desiccant is a substance which absorbs moisture. Sand, alum, cornmeal, starch, detergent powders, borax powder and silica gel are all desiccants. However, a desiccant used for plant preservation must not only absorb moisture but absorb it quickly, to enable the natural colouring of the plant material to be retained. A slow preserving process usually results in loss of colour.

The two products which I have used with the greatest success are silica gel and borax powder, but, as with all products, it is advisable to experiment for yourself, particularly as the conditions under which you preserve must also be taken into consideration. As a guide for readers who have no previous experience with desiccants, I will explain the advantages and disadvantages of silica gel and borax.

SILICA GEL

Silica gel, which absorbs up to 50 per cent of its own weight in moisture, is used industrially for moisture absorption. It looks rather like granulated sugar. Silica gel is more expensive than borax, but it has the advantage that, unlike borax, it does not demand heat during use.

It is often difficult to obtain a suitable grade of crystals, as the standard grade sold by chemists and drug stores is usually too large and heavy, and would cause delicate plant materials to become distorted. The intense hardness of these crystals makes them unsuitable for crushing, even in an electric grinder, so it is best to buy crystals sold specifically for the purpose of preserving plant material. These are sold under a variety of trade names and usually contain silica gel of a more refined grade than the standard crystals. On account of the difficulty I myself have experienced in locating and recommending retail sources for preserving crystals, I now market my own brand of crystals (see page 156).

Silica gel and preserving crystals should always be stored in an airtight tin to keep them dry.

From time to time crystals will become fully charged with their maximum amount of moisture. They will not actually feel wet, and different brands of crystals show their moisture content in different ways, so always check the instructions given with the crystals you are using. The most usual indication is a colour change. For example, the flower crystals I market lose their blue colouring and become a dirty pink. When this happens the crystals can be reactivated as follows. Pour the crystals into a shallow pan and put them in a warm oven at 120°C (250°F/Gas Mark $\frac{1}{2}$). Stir them occasionally to ensure even drying. After fifteen to thirty minutes, the blue colour will reappear, indicating that the crystals are dry. Turn off the heat and leave the crystals in the oven for a further half-hour or so to cool slightly. Then return them to their storage tin. Replace the lid of the tin immediately, before the crystals start to absorb any moisture from the air. Do not attempt to preserve flowers in the crystals until they are quite cold. If they are reactivated in this way when necessary, silica gel crystals can be used over and over again and will last for an indefinite period.

BORAX

Household borax is a powder obtainable relatively inexpensively from chemists and drug stores. It does, however, have certain disadvantages. During use a constant dry heat of approximately 24°C (75°F) must be maintained to obtain successful results. Borax also has a tendency to cling and the specks of powder are particularly noticeable on dark-coloured materials. These particles can be brushed off fairly easily, however. Again, many flowers, particularly roses, will not preserve successfully in borax. Having been gathered at a partially open stage of growth, they will have exceptionally solid centres. Borax will not draw out the moisture as efficiently and rapidly as silica gel, which usually means they will turn brown. Borax can be stored anywhere dry. A cardboard box or a paper bag makes a perfectly adequate container. When you use borax, however, do make sure it is completely dry. Unless it is quite dry and free from lumps, plant materials will not preserve successfully. The powder should run through your fingers like table salt. If it clings together and is inclined to be lumpy, spread it out on a shallow tray and leave it in a warm place, such as an airing cupboard, to dry.

PRESERVING FLOWERS IN A DESICCANT

To avoid that typically dried look in a flower arrangement, the two characteristics to aim for are colour impact and the retention of each flower's natural form. Some flowers in Chapter 1, together with the everlasting flowers in Chapter 1, can be preserved by the air method, but other garden and florists' flowers need the aid of a desiccant to preserve their shape, form and colour. It is difficult to put into words the charm of, for example, three preserved water lilies casually arranged in a glass dish in mid-winter, or a single peony arranged with its own foliage to emphasise its intricate beauty. It is often not necessary to preserve more than, say seven, flowers by this method to create a feature in an arrangement of other dried and preserved plant material. These examples also illustrate that, for the beginner, and often for those with experience in flower arranging too, restraint is the keynote in the use of desiccant-preserved flowers. This is fortunate, as, if you preserve too many flowers, you will almost certainly find that you have storage problems. Remember, it is much better to have a smaller collection of preserved flowers that can be properly stored and cared for than large quantities that become squashed and damaged because the storage space is inadequate.

CHOOSING SUITABLE FLOWERS

I find that the beginner often wants to preserve the flowers that are the least suitable for preserving. You will observe that evergreen leaves have a much firmer structure than deciduous ones. Well, flowers are much the same, some flower petals have a much stronger and firmer tissue structure than others. I would advise concentrating on these to begin with. When you feel confident in the techniques, you can experiment with more delicate blooms. With experience, one becomes able to judge the chances of success just by looking at and feeling the petals of a flower. The flowers illustrated in Chapter 1 will serve as a useful guide to those flowers which can be preserved successfully.

fig. 12

If you want perfect desiccant-preserved flowers, I am afraid you must be prepared to sacrifice their all-too-short lives as fresh flowers, as it is most important to gather them before they begin to develop seedpods. When this stage is reached in the life cycle of a flower, although at a glance it may look perfect, the petals are in fact either beginning to fade or loosen in preparation for falling off. If the petals are at all loose, they will almost certainly fall off after preserving. Many large-petalled flowers, such as roses, preserve far more successfully if picked before they are fully open. Figure 12 shows a rose just ready to be picked for preserving. Figure 13 shows the stage at which a bloom is likely to shatter when preserved. If, however, for some reason a flower needs to be preserved at the loose-petalled stage, with patience it is possible to glue the petals carefully back on (see page 150).

fig. 13

The ideal flowers for preserving are those picked fresh from the garden. They should be gathered when dry, without any trace of dew or rain. Even flowers that appear dry on the surface often retain moisture deep down between their petals—this is frequently the case with roses. A good shake will reveal any hidden moisture. Flowers preserved when wet will inevitably turn brown.

Do not gather flowers at midday in full sun during hot weather, as the petals will then be limp and their formation cannot be satisfactorily retained—petals must be firm, rigid and crisp if they are to hold their shape while covered with a desiccant. One of the main reasons for loss of form in preserved flowers is the attempt to preserve those which are showing signs of wilting. Discard any flowers marred by insect holes, distorted petals, unsightly marks or bruises (often a result of wind or rain damage), loss of colour, or scorching caused by sun bleaching. If for some reason you cannot preserve flowers as soon as they are picked, re-cut the stems, to ensure an intake of water and immediately stand them in water. Keep them in the water until you can preserve them, but remember that flowers left in water for any length of time will continue to open.

TRANSPORTING FRESH FLOWERS FOR PRESERVING

Although, ideally, flowers should be taken directly from the garden to the preserving tin, naturally this is not always possible, particularly for those without a garden, who have to rely on visits to friends' gardens, or florists. Flowers can usually be kept fresh and firm enough to withstand a journey if they are either stood in a container of water or water-retaining flower foam, or carefully placed in a refrigerator bag or box, provided that they are adequately protected from the moisture of the ice pack. Although flowers must be kept fresh, they must also be kept dry, so it is unwise to pack them in a polythene bag as the moisture that forms on the inside of the bag will condense on the flowers.

REVIVING WILTED FRESH FLOWERS

Should it be necessary to preserve flowers that have already wilted, they can often be revived by conditioning (a firming process). Fill a container with very warm to hot, but not boiling, water. Re-cut the flower stems and immediately plunge the ends into the water. Let the flowers stand for several hours in a cool place. If, for some reason, you have had to pick flowers that ideally need to open a little more, they can be treated in the same way, but watch them carefully. Do not leave them overnight as they may open too much while you sleep.

A WORD OF WARNING

Do not expect to be able to store flowers in a freezer until you have time to preserve them—you may have heard or read of freeze-drying, but that is something completely different; it is a specialised process requiring elaborate equipment not generally available to the amateur. We all know how dahlias in the garden look after the first hard autumn frost. Well, this is exactly what your flowers will be like a little while after you remove them from the freezer. You may argue, as many a telephone caller has with me, that you have put them in the freezer, and they look fine. Yes, I agree, they will look perfect while they are still frozen, but when you remove them and allow them to thaw out, you can expect to encounter a soggy mass.

COLOUR CHANGES IN DESICCANT-PRESERVED FLOWERS

Some flowers develop slight colour changes during the preserving process and while some preserved flowers stand the test of time displayed in an arrangement, others mellow or literally fade. Personally, I think it is fun just to accept any colour change that may occur during the preserving of garden flowers. A preserved flower arrangement can be as full of colour as an arrangement of fresh flowers, but if, for every flower in a preserved arrangement, an identical flower was picked for a fresh arrangement and then the two arrangements were compared, the over-all colour effect would be different. The preservation process can intensify the strength of colour in some flowers while weakening it in others. If you start with, say, a red or a yellow flower, after preserving you will still have a red or yellow flower, but the tone of the colour may have changed, so the tonal value of the preserved arrangement will differ from that of the fresh arrangement. For me this adds interest and excitement to preserving. And, after all, the tone of fresh flowers in the garden changes between the bud stage and the fully mature flower, and according to the degree and strength of sunlight.

STABILITY OF COLOUR

It would be very convenient if I were able to list the colours that, under perfect conditions, remain stable for months or even years after preserving, but to attempt this could cause total frustration. For example, let us look at blue flowers. Delphiniums, cornflowers and forget-me-nots appear to retain their true colour indefinitely—I have some that are now fifteen years old and still good. I find, however, that a blue campanula will fade to white after only a month or so. Pink flowers, in general, lose their colour intensity after a few months, at which time they are lovely to use in soft, subdued colour schemes. Red appears to be unpredictable, but, in fact, shades of red basically fall into two groups: orange or yellow reds last well and should be used when a clear, bright red is required; blue-reds, that is magenta, rose or pinky reds, tend to darken considerably as the blue undertone is accentuated. Most yellow flowers, I find, are very reliable. Many white flowers tend to turn cream, which is really very pleasing as cream is not so dominant when arranged with other colours.

PRESERVING LEAVES IN DESICCANT

The glycerine method is usually considered the obvious way to preserve foliage, but although this method produces beautifully pliable leaves, its use is restricted to fully mature leaves. Immature leaves will not preserve successfully by the glycerine method, nor will leaves which have begun to develop their autumn colours. Glycerine preserving always produces a fairly marked change in the colouring of the leaves. As we have discussed, this can be an advantage, as the different colours produced by preserving extend the range of colours available to the arranger. However, if you want to retain the natural colouring of the leaves, you must use the desiccant method. There are four groups of leaves in which the retention of the natural colourings may be particularly desirable. These are leaves which have developed their autumn colours; immature leaves; silver leaves, and leaves which have beautiful markings or veining. I find that, in general, it is thin-textured deciduous leaves that are best suited to desiccant preserving. Evergreen leaves do not, on the whole, preserve well by this method. Variegated ivy leaves are an exception, but even with these it is a good idea to preserve more than you need: I rarely get 100 per cent success. With variegated ivy, it is advisable to pick mature leaves, as the immature ones are usually more fleshy. Remember, all desiccant-preserved leaves are fragile and therefore require careful handling. The special spray coating recommended for flowers on page 149 is ideal for use on smooth-surfaced, desiccant-preserved leaves, rendering them more pliable. It also gives them a sheen, a great advantage in our attempt to create preserved arrangements with a fresh look.

THE DESICCANT METHOD OF PRESERVING

CONTAINERS FOR PRESERVING

For flower preservation with silica gel or preserving crystals, gather together a selection of airtight tins in different shapes and sizes. It is often possible to buy large, empty biscuit or sweet tins at confectioners' or big stores for a nominal sum, especially at Christmas time. Small tins, particularly round ground-coffee tins, are useful for preserving individual blooms. For borax preserving, you will need open cardboard boxes, so collect empty boxes, such as shoe boxes and chocolate and writing-paper boxes.

It is very important that the correct type of container is used. To prepare your container, spoon desiccant into the bottom of the tin or box to form a layer approximately 12 mm ($\frac{1}{2}$ in) deep (fig. 14).

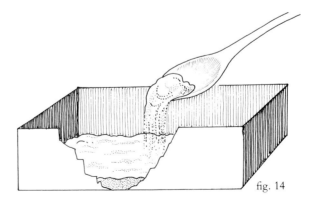

fig. 14

IS IT NECESSARY TO WIRE FLOWERS AND LEAVES BEFORE PRESERVING?

FLOWERS

Some flowers, such as delphiniums, have stems which will remain firm and rigid after preservation. It would be ideal if all flowers were like this, but many, such as dahlias and water lilies, for example, have very succulent stems, which will collapse when the moisture is drawn out, and they need to have their stems replaced by florists' wires (fig. 15). Other flowers, such as roses, which appear to have stiff stems, tend to develop a weakness just under the flower head which causes the head to flop over after preserving. This problem can be overcome by cutting the flower to about 40 mm ($1\frac{1}{2}$ in) of stem and pushing a wire up into the stem to reinforce it (fig. 16). The best wires to use are 20-gauge, but, if these are difficult to obtain, wires of a similar thickness will do. It is important to wire flowers before preserving. During the preserving process the sap in the flower will cause corrosion of the wire, and this, together with the slight shrinkage of the flower, will ensure that, when the flower is preserved, the wire will remain firm and secure. At this stage it is only necessary to have a short length of wire (50 mm/2 in or so). It is easier to fit flowers with short wires into preserving tins, and they are also easier to handle during the preserving process and to store. When you are ready to arrange the flowers, the wire can be lengthened as shown on page 150.

fig. 15

fig. 16

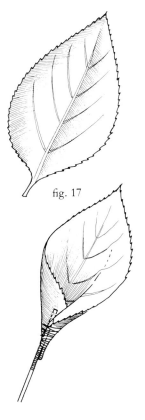

fig. 17

LEAVES

Individual soft leaves, such as rose leaves which have a naturally flattish habit of growth, can be coaxed into a more interesting form by wiring. Mould the leaf tightly around a short length of wire and bind it with fine silver wire, as shown in figure 17. This can only be attempted before the leaves are preserved while they are supple and can be manipulated easily without damage. After preserving, the wire can be lengthened as shown on page 151.

POSITIONING FLOWERS

I recommend that the beginner should only attempt to preserve one layer of flowers in each tin, to avoid the risk of damage. It is also advisable for the beginner to restrict each batch to one type of flower, to make it easier to calculate preserving times.

1. A face-down position (fig. 18(a)) is generally best for simple flowers with flat faces, such as daisies, which are the ideal type of flower for the beginner's first experiments. Clusters and sprays of florets should also be positioned in this way.

2. A face-up position (fig. 18(b)) is the most successful position for rounded double flowers and is particularly suitable for roses. It is also an alternative method for flat-faced flowers which are only partially open (fig. 18(c)).

3. Flowers which are trumpet- or bell-shaped (individual hollyhock flowers, for example) should be positioned on their sides (fig. 18(d)).

4. Flower spikes, such as those of the delphinium, with florets encircling the entire stem, need a little extra protection if the florets are not to be crushed. An effective method is to bend two strips of thin cardboard tent-fashioned, cut notches in them and place them in the bottom of the tin. The flower spikes can then be laid across the cardboard tent shapes, with their stems held in the notches (fig. 18(e)).

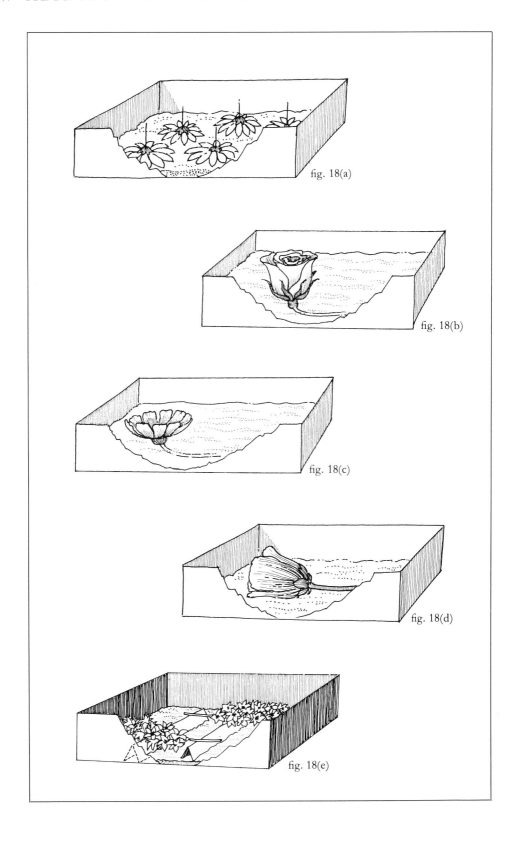

fig. 18(a)

fig. 18(b)

fig. 18(c)

fig. 18(d)

fig. 18(e)

POSITIONING LEAVES

Because leaves are less intricate in their formation than flowers, it is easy to preserve several layers in a single tin; however, each layer of leaves must be covered with about 12 mm ($\frac{1}{2}$ in) of desiccant before the next layer is positioned (fig. 19).

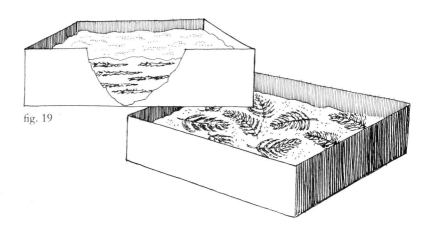

fig. 19

COVERING THE FLOWERS

Using a large spoon, sprinkle the preserving crystals or silica gel slowly and carefully round each flower. Never sprinkle crystals on top of a flower, as the instant weight would destroy the flower's natural form. As you continue sprinkling, the crystals will cover the flowers (fig. 20). Do not try to poke or force crystals in between the petals, this is not necessary and would cause damage and distortion. Exceptions to this rule are trumpet- or bell-shaped flowers, which should have their centres filled with crystals before crystals are sprinkled round them.

When the flowers are completely covered with a layer of crystals about 12 mm ($\frac{1}{2}$ in) deep on top, replace the lid of the tin (fig. 21). If the lid is not completely airtight, seal it with sticky tape.

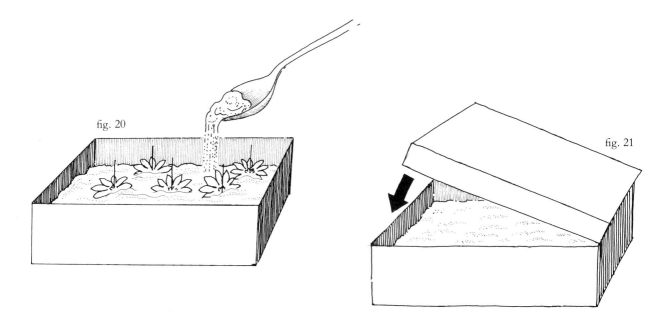

fig. 20

fig. 21

BORAX

It is a good idea to sift borax over the flowers through a sieve, to disperse any remaining lumps in the powder (fig. 22). You can sift the borax on top of the flowers as, unlike crystals, borax will not crush them. If you prefer to spoon the borax on in the same way as preserving crystals, sieve it immediately before use. Again, the flowers should be covered with a 12 mm ($\frac{1}{2}$ in) layer (fig. 23). When the plant materials are completely covered, place the box, without a lid, where a constant temperature of 24°C (75°F) can be maintained—a heated airing cupboard is ideal.

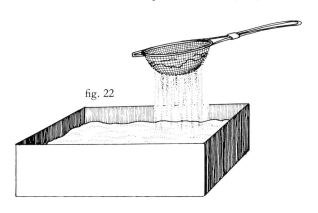

fig. 22

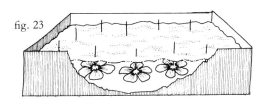

fig. 23

MARKING

It is essential that each tin or box should be clearly marked with its contents and the date. Failure to do this invariably causes chaos, especially if several batches are being preserved at different times. The length of time the flowers take to preserve will depend on the size, density and thickness of their petals. Many tiny flowers used in miniature arrangements only take two or three days, but larger flowers, such as roses and dahlias, take a week to ten days. Most will be preserved within two weeks, although very fleshy flowers, such as orchids, will take longer.

REMOVING FLOWERS

Before attempting to uncover the complete batch, it is advisable to scrape back the desiccant gently and remove one flower. Hold the flower to your ear and give it a gentle flick; if it is ready, it will sound crisp and papery. The remaining flowers can then be removed by carefully pouring off the desiccant, letting it fall slowly through your fingers; this will enable you to catch each flower in turn and carefully remove it by its stem (fig. 24). Stand the preserved flowers in a container or block of flower foam (fig. 25). Never pile them in a heap on the table.

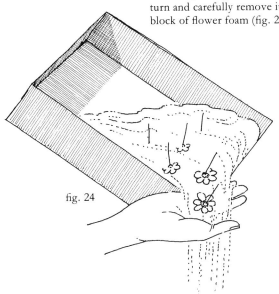

fig. 24

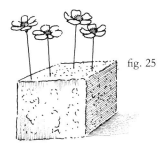

fig. 25

GROOMING

If specially prepared and selected crystals are used, these should fall away from most flowers as each one is removed from the tin, leaving the surface of the petals completely clean. A quick flick on the stem is all that is necessary to remove any residue. Flowers with tiny hairs or rough surfaces in their centres may retain some particles, but these can easily be brushed away with a soft paintbrush (fig. 26). A brush will also remove any clinging particles of borax.

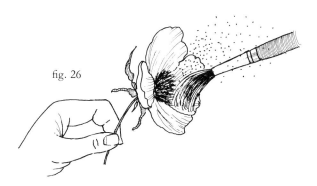

fig. 26

DEALING WITH FALLING PETALS

When flowers, particularly of single-flowered varieties, are removed from the desiccant, the occasional petal will break off at the joint. If a dab of quick-drying contact adhesive is applied to the base of the petal, it can be fixed securely back in place with little effort. Petals with very pointed bases can be attached more firmly if the bases are trimmed as shown in figure 27 before they are glued back. When moisture is removed from a flower, there is always a slight shrinkage, which is usually most noticeable in single flowers and flowers with large petals. This means that petals which do not overlap become slightly spaced. It is advisable to give the petals a little artificial support by glueing them one to another, as shown in figure 28.

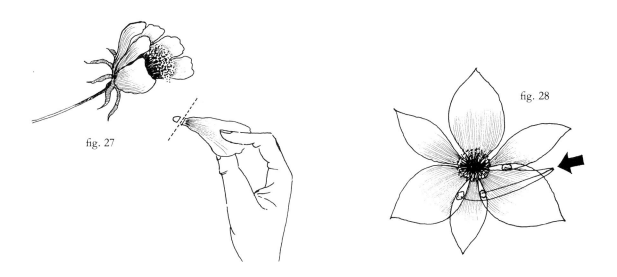

fig. 27

fig. 28

THE REACTION OF DESICCANT-PRESERVED FLOWERS TO A DAMP ATMOSOPHERE

Flowers differ so much in structure and texture that it is really only when the arranger has preserved and handled many different types that a knowledge is acquired of how different flowers withstand damp weather conditions. Flowers suitable for preserving by the air method (see page 136) are usually unaffected, as are many desiccant-preserved flowers, particularly those with especially

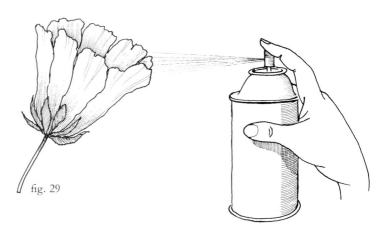

fig. 29

tough-textured petals or those, such as Pompon and Decorative type dahlias, with small, closely packed, overlapping petals. Flowers with large petals are generally inclined to flop, although, again, much depends on the texture of the petals. In general, it is essential that desiccant-preserved flowers should be kept as dry as possible. Damp is a hazard I all too often have to contend with when transporting flower arrangements between my home and flower arrangement societies on a wet day. The encounters with the elements during packing and unpacking the car can spell disaster to the most carefully preserved flowers. Within the home, conditions are not so extreme, but you must avoid placing flowers in a room known to be damp. Even in centrally heated rooms, flowers susceptible to reabsorption of air moisture can be vulnerable during damp weather conditions in summer, when the heating is turned off. A coating of a specially prepared spray (fig. 29) can be very helpful for problem flowers, but it must only be applied to flowers when they are completely dry, that is, either as soon as the flowers are removed from the desiccant or taken from the storage tin (see page 156 for details of a suitable spray). It is important that the directions on such products should be carefully observed, as too heavy an application of spray can have a more disastrous effect than the damp weather conditions. When correctly applied the spray can also improve the flower visibly, giving the petals a natural-looking sheen without making them too shiny. Varnish can also be used to give protection from damp. It is a matter of choice, but I feel varnish gives the flowers a very artificial look. Never attempt to mix desiccant-preserved flowers with fresh foliage. This would mean that the flowers had to stand in water or a water-retaining material, which would be disastrous for them.

STORAGE

Once flowers have been preserved, they can be kept in absolutely perfect condition for many months if they are properly stored. Desiccant-preserved flowers should be stored either in flower foam in containers on the top shelf of a heated airing cupboard, or, alternatively, in sealed airtight tins. As a safety measure, before placing flowers in a tin, sprinkle a layer of dry desiccant in the bottom to absorb any air moisture in the tin, and also any moisture that may still remain deep in the centres of the flowers.

Cut strips of cardboard and pierce them with holes large enough to hold the flower stems. Glue the strips across the tin, as shown in figure 30, and slip the flower stems through the holes. Replace the airtight lid—if you are in any doubt about whether the lid is completely airtight, it is advisable to seal it with sticky tape. Remember to mark the outside to indicate its contents. Store the tin in any convenient place where there is no danger of it being knocked over.

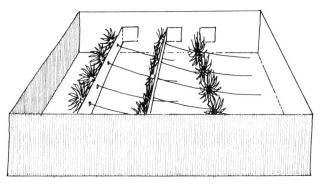

fig. 30

LENGTHENING STEMS OF FLOWERS, FOLIAGE AND CONES

Flowers Unlike fresh flowers, which have to be arranged with whatever length of stem they happen to have, dried and preserved flowers can have their stems lengthened. This is particularly useful as a means of using individual flowers such as hollyhocks (see page 00) which have less than 12 mm ($\frac{1}{2}$ in) of natural stem. It is also useful to be able to re-use flowers when the stems have been cut short for previous arrangements. The heads of flowers such as hydrangeas are often much too large for an arrangement, but their branched formation enables each head to be divided to provide many smaller flower heads (see fig. 31), and the stems of these will also need to be lengthened. Flowers that are preserved in a desiccant need to be wired before preservation. Instructions for this preliminary wiring are given on page 145. For practical reasons only short wires are used at this initial stage, but, before the flowers can be used in an arrangement, the wires will usually need to be lengthened.

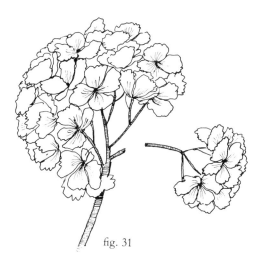

fig. 31

fig. 32

WIRE STEMS

Extending flower stems with wires has the added advantage of enabling you to bend each stem to the angle at which you wish to use it in an arrangement. Various lengths and gauges of wire are usually obtainable from florists or floral art suppliers, making it easy to select fine gauge wires for small flowers and coarser gauge wires for larger flowers. Secure the wire to the flower's existing natural or wire stem with fine silver rose wire (see fig. 32) which is available both in cut lengths and on a reel.

I find that some individual flowers can look more attractive and are more effective in an arrangement when they are assembled into sprays. Take two or three flowers which are already wired and attach each one at intervals to a long central wire (see fig. 33).

fig. 33

fig. 34

fig. 35

NATURAL PLANT STEMS

The alternative way of lengthening stems is to make use of the stems of other plants. Here use the stems of grasses for small light-weight flowers. For heavier flowers, the stalks of many herbaceous plants are ideal, providing, of course, that these are hollow. I gather them at the end of the year when they have become dry, with an almost woody texture, and store them in a box to ensure that a constant supply of extension stems are always to hand. To attach the flower to its extension stem, dab a blob of glue on the flower's existing stem and carefully insert it into the hollow stalk (see fig. 34).

Foliage   Leaves that already have a short length of stem, or have had preliminary wiring as described on page 146 can be extended in the same way as that described for flowers. If, however, the leaf has little or no stem, which often happens when it is necessary to take and use individual leaves from a branch of foliage, then I find it easier to wire them as shown in figure 35.

Interesting effects can be achieved in an arrangement by making up your own sprays of leaves from individual leaves. The process is very easy (see fig. 36(a) and (b)) and as you can see leaves are bound individually to a central heavy-gauge wire. The great advantage of these leaf sprays is that each one can be bent to whatever angle is required.

fig. 36(a)

fig. 36(b)

Cones Cones of all sizes can be wired to provide interesting flower-like forms for use in arrangements. Choose a suitable gauge of wire for each size of cone. This is of particular importance with really large heavy cones, as the wire must be thick enough to provide a firm rigid stem and to prevent the cone from collapsing under its own weight. If necessary use two wires together for greater strength.

fig. 37(a)

Bend the wire in half and thread it between the bottom two rows of scales (fig. 37(a)). Pull the wire taut and it will become embedded between the cone scales. Twist the two ends tightly together and then twist them round the little nodule of the cone's natural stem. Continue twisting the ends round each other to form an extended stem (fig. 37(b)). Some cones or part cones, such as the cedar cone centres, cannot be wired as I have described because of the formation of their scales. Cones such as this can be stuck with a blob of glue into the top of a strong hollow stem (fig. 37(c)).

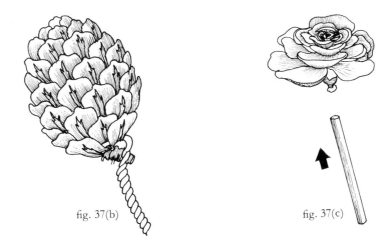

fig. 37(b)   fig. 37(c)

Binding stems   Both wire and natural stems of flowers, leaves and cones will require binding if you are to achieve perfection in your finished work. This is particularly important for competitive work. Binding not only hides the join, but, with wire stems, it provides smooth wire with a firmer means of anchorage in an arrangement. For this job I use gutta-percha tape which is a narrow plastic tape sold by florists and is made in white, brown and green. Personally I prefer always to use the brown tape as I find its earthy colouring less obtrusive. Whichever type of stem you are binding, hold one end of the tape round the stem with the thumb and forefinger of your left hand and begin twisting with this thumb and finger, using your right hand to hold and guide the tape at a downward angle, as shown in figure 38. When the stem is completely covered, break the tape and press it firmly round the base of the stem which will enable it to stick to itself and provide a natural seal.

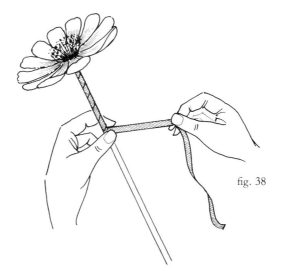

fig. 38

LIST OF SUPPLIERS

BRITAIN
Flower Preserving Crystals and Protective Spray, send
stamped addressed envelope to :
77 Bulbridge Road,
Wilton,
Salisbury,
Wiltshire
SP2 0LE

USA
Roberta Moffit,
P.O. Box 3597
Wilmington
DE 19807

INDEX

Please note that numbers in roman refer to page numbers, and those in *italic* refer to pages on which illustrations appear.